Unlock

Second Edition | **3**

Reading, Writing & Critical Thinking

STUDENT'S BOOK WITH DIGITAL PACK

Carolyn Westbrook and Lida Baker
with Chris Sowton, Jennifer Farmer
and Janet Gokay

CAMBRIDGE UNIVERSITY PRESS

CAMBRIDGE
UNIVERSITY PRESS & ASSESSMENT

Shaftesbury Road, Cambridge CB2 8EA, United Kingdom

One Liberty Plaza, 20th Floor, New York, NY 10006, USA

477 Williamstown Road, Port Melbourne, VIC 3207, Australia

314–321, 3rd Floor, Plot 3, Splendor Forum, Jasola District Centre, New Delhi – 110025, India

103 Penang Road, #05-06/07, Visioncrest Commercial, Singapore 238467

Cambridge University Press & Assessment is a department of the University of Cambridge.

We share the University's mission to contribute to society through the pursuit of education, learning and research at the highest international levels of excellence.

www.cambridge.org
Information on this title: www.cambridge.org/9781009031400

© Cambridge University Press & Assessment 2019

This publication is in copyright. Subject to statutory exception and to the provisions of relevant collective licensing agreements, no reproduction of any part may take place without the written permission of Cambridge University Press & Assessment.

First published 2014
Second Edition 2019
Second Edition update published 2021

20 19 18 17 16 15 14

Printed in the Netherlands by Wilco BV

A catalogue record for this publication is available from the British Library

ISBN 978-1-009-03140-0 Reading, Writing and Critical Thinking Student's Book with Digital Pack 3
ISBN 978-1-009-03130-1 Reading, Writing and Critical Thinking Student's eBook with Digital Pack 3

Cambridge University Press & Assessment has no responsibility for the persistence or accuracy of URLs for external or third-party internet websites referred to in this publication, and does not guarantee that any content on such websites is, or will remain, accurate or appropriate. Information regarding prices, travel timetables, and other factual information given in this work is correct at the time of first printing but Cambridge University Press & Assessment does not guarantee the accuracy of such information thereafter.

CONTENTS

Map of the book		4
Your guide to *Unlock*		8
UNIT 1	Animals	14
UNIT 2	The environment	36
UNIT 3	Transport	58
UNIT 4	Customs and traditions	80
UNIT 5	Health and fitness	102
UNIT 6	Discovery and invention	124
UNIT 7	Fashion	146
UNIT 8	Economics	168
Glossary		190
Video scripts		202
Acknowledgements		207
Unlock Second Edition Advisory Panel		208

MAP OF THE BOOK

UNIT	VIDEO	READING	VOCABULARY
1 ANIMALS Reading 1: Endangered species (Ecology / Zoology) Reading 2: Losing the battle for survival (Ecology / Zoology)	Great egret and dolphin fishing	*Key reading skill:* Reading for main ideas in academic texts *Additional skills:* Understanding key vocabulary Using your knowledge Reading for detail Working out meaning from context Predicting content using visuals Summarizing Making inferences Synthesizing	Academic verbs
2 THE ENVIRONMENT Reading 1: Our changing planet (Environmental science / Natural science) Reading 2: The causes and effects of deforestation (Environmental science / Natural science)	Colorado River, Grand Canyon, Yosemite	*Key reading skills:* Reading for detail Identifying purpose and audience *Additional skills:* Understanding key vocabulary Predicting content using visuals Previewing Reading for main ideas Scanning to find information Summarizing Making inferences Synthesizing	Academic vocabulary Environment collocations
3 TRANSPORT Reading 1: Masdar: City of the future (Transport management / Urban planning) Reading 2: An essay about traffic congestion (Transport management / Urban planning)	The jumbo jet	*Key reading skill:* Predicting content using visuals *Additional skills:* Understanding key vocabulary Reading for main ideas Reading for detail Making inferences Synthesizing	Transport collocations Synonyms for verbs
4 CUSTOMS AND TRADITIONS Reading 1: Customs around the world (Cultural studies / Sociology) Reading 2: Protecting our intangible cultural heritage (Cultural studies / Sociology / Anthropology)	South Korean Coming of Age Day	*Key reading skills:* Annotating a text Previewing a text *Additional skills:* Understanding key vocabulary Using your knowledge Reading for main ideas Reading for detail Making inferences Synthesizing	Synonyms to avoid repetition

GRAMMAR	CRITICAL THINKING	WRITING
Comparative adjectives *Grammar for writing:* Word order Combining sentences with *and, or, but, whereas, both, neither*	Comparing and contrasting facts	*Academic writing skill:* Writing topic sentences *Writing task:* Complete a comparison-and-contrast essay.
Grammar for writing: Verbs of cause and effect *Because* and *because of*	Analyzing cause and effect	*Academic writing skills:* Understanding paragraph unity Writing supporting sentences and details Giving examples *Writing task:* Complete a cause-and-effect essay.
Making suggestions *Grammar for writing:* First conditional *If ... not* and *unless*	Evaluating solutions to a problem	*Academic writing skill:* Writing a concluding sentence *Writing task:* Complete a problem–solution essay.
Avoiding generalizations Adverbs of frequency to avoid generalizations *Grammar for writing:* Paraphrasing	Responding to an author's ideas	*Academic writing skill:* Writing a summary and a personal response *Writing task:* Write a summary paragraph and a response paragraph.

UNIT	VIDEO	READING	VOCABULARY
5 HEALTH AND FITNESS Reading 1: An article about exercise and keeping fit (Health science) Reading 2: An essay about whose responsibility it is to fight obesity (Nutrition)	Sugar survey supports labelling on food and drinks	*Key reading skill:* Making inferences *Additional skills:* Understanding key vocabulary Predicting content using visuals Using your knowledge Skimming Reading for main ideas Reading for detail Scanning to predict content Synthesizing	Health and fitness collocations
6 DISCOVERY AND INVENTION Reading 1: The magic of mimicry (Mechanical engineering / Industrial design) Reading 2: The world of tomorrow (Mechanical engineering / Industrial design)	China's man-made river	*Key reading skill:* Scanning to find information *Additional skills:* Understanding key vocabulary Using your knowledge Reading for main ideas Annotating Making inferences Reading for detail Synthesizing	Prefixes
7 FASHION Reading 1: Is *fast fashion* taking over? (Fashion design / Retail management / Business) Reading 2: Offshore production (Fashion design / Retail management / Business)	Savile Row's first female Master Tailor	*Key reading skill:* Distinguishing fact from opinion *Additional skills:* Understanding key vocabulary Using your knowledge Reading for main ideas Reading for detail Making inferences Skimming Scanning to find information Synthesizing	Vocabulary for the fashion business
8 ECONOMICS Reading 1: How should you invest your money? (Business / Economics) Reading 2: Falling income, rising expenditure (Business / Economics)	The stock market crash of 1929	*Key reading skill:* Skimming for general ideas *Additional skills:* Understanding key vocabulary Using your knowledge Reading for main ideas Reading for detail Making inferences Annotating Synthesizing	Vocabulary for economics and economic trends

GRAMMAR	CRITICAL THINKING	WRITING
Verb and noun forms *Grammar for writing:* Stating opinions Stating a purpose Linking contrasting sentences	Supporting an argument	*Academic writing skill:* Structuring an essay (introductory, body and concluding paragraphs) *Writing task:* Write a balanced opinion essay.
Making predictions with modals and adverbs of certainty *Grammar for writing:* Relative clauses Prepositional phrases with advantages and disadvantages	Analyzing advantages and disadvantages	*Academic writing skill:* Writing an introductory paragraph (hook, background information, thesis statement) *Writing task:* Write an explanatory essay.
Grammar for writing: Multi-word prepositions to combine information	Identifying strong arguments	*Academic writing skills:* Using body paragraphs in point–counterpoint essays Using counter-arguments Using cohesion *Writing task:* Write a point–counterpoint essay.
Grammar for writing: Describing graphs using noun and verb phrases Prepositions and conjunctions to add data Using approximations	Understanding and interpreting line graphs	*Academic writing skills:* Writing a description of a graph Writing a concluding paragraph *Writing task:* Write an analysis essay.

YOUR GUIDE TO UNLOCK

Unlock your academic potential

Unlock Second Edition is a six-level, academic-light English course created to build the skills and language students need for their studies (CEFR Pre-A1 to C1). It develops students' ability to think critically in an academic context right from the start of their language learning. Every level has 100% new inspiring video on a range of academic topics.

Confidence in teaching.

Joy in learning.

Better Learning WITH UNLOCK SECOND EDITION

Better Learning is our simple approach where insights we've gained from research have helped shape content that drives results. We've listened to teachers all around the world and made changes so that Unlock Second Edition better supports students along the way to academic success.

CRITICAL THINKING

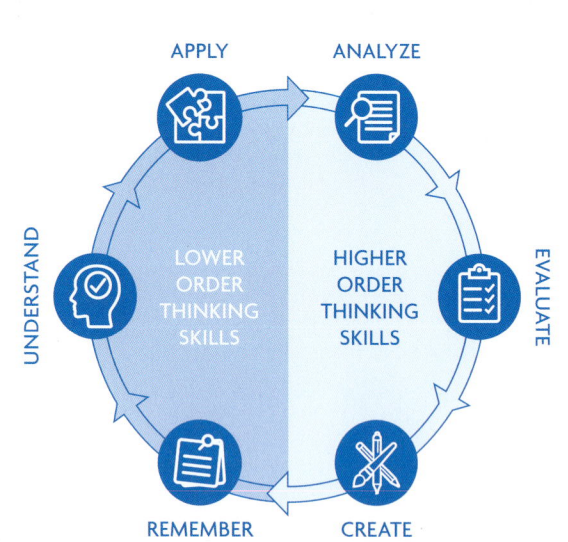

Critical thinking in Unlock Second Edition …

- is **informed** by a range of academic research from Bloom in the 1950s, to Krathwohl and Anderson in the 2000s, to more recent considerations relating to 21st Century Skills
- has a **refined** syllabus with a better mix of higher- and lower-order critical thinking skills
- is **measurable**, with objectives and self-evaluation so students can track their critical thinking progress
- is **transparent** so teachers and students know when and why they're developing critical thinking skills
- is **supported** with professional development material for teachers so teachers can teach with confidence

… so that students have the best possible chance of academic success.

INSIGHT
Most classroom time is currently spent on developing lower-order critical thinking skills. Students need to be able to use higher-order critical thinking skills too.

CONTENT
Unlock Second Edition includes the right mix of lower- and higher-order thinking skills development in every unit, with clear learning objectives.

RESULTS
Students are better prepared for their academic studies and have the confidence to apply the critical thinking skills they have developed.

DIGITAL CLASSROOM MATERIAL

The *Unlock* Second Edition Digital Classroom Material …

- offers extra, **motivating** practice in speaking, critical thinking and language
- provides a **convenient** bank of language and skills reference informed by our exclusive Corpus research
- is easily **accessible** and **navigable** from students' mobile phones
- is fully **integrated** into every unit
- provides Unlock-**specific** activities to extend the lesson whenever you see this symbol

… so that students can easily get the right, extra practice they need, when they need it.

INSIGHT
The digital classroom material is most effective when it's an integral, well-timed part of a lesson.

CONTENT
Every unit of *Unlock* Second Edition is enhanced with bespoke digital classroom material to extend the skills and language students are learning in the book. The symbol shows when to use the material.

RESULTS
Students are motivated by having relevant extension material on their mobile phones to maximize their language learning. Teachers are reassured that the material adds real language-learning value to their lessons.

RESEARCH

We have gained deeper insights to inform *Unlock* Second Edition by …

- carrying out **extensive market research** with teachers and students to fully understand their needs throughout the course's development
- consulting **academic research** into critical thinking
- refining our vocabulary syllabus using our **exclusive Corpus research**

… so that you can be assured of the quality of *Unlock* Second Edition.

INSIGHT
- Consultation with global Advisory Panel
- Comprehensive reviews of material
- Face-to-face interviews and Skype™ calls
- Classroom observations

CONTENT
- Improved critical thinking
- 100% new video and video lessons
- Clearer contexts for language presentation and practice
- Text-by-text glossaries
- More supportive writing sections
- Digital workbook with more robust content
- Comprehensive teacher support

RESULTS
"Thank you for all the effort you've put into developing Unlock Second Edition. As far as I can see, I think the new edition is more academic and more appealing to young adults."

Burçin Gönülsen,
Işık Üniversity, Turkey

HOW UNLOCK WORKS

Unlock your knowledge
Encourages discussion around the themes of the unit with inspiration from interesting questions and striking images.

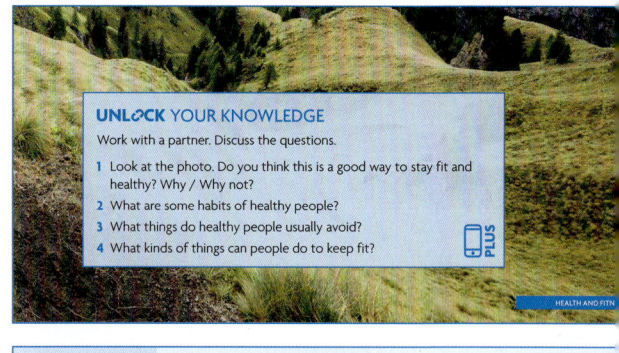

Watch and listen
Features an engaging and motivating video which generates interest in the topic and develops listening skills.

READING

Reading 1
The first text offers students the opportunity to develop the reading skills required to process academic texts, and presents and practises the vocabulary needed to comprehend the text itself.

Reading 2
Presents a second text which provides a different angle on the topic and serves as a model text for the writing task.

Language development
Consolidates and expands on the language presented in preparation for the writing task.

HOW *UNLOCK* WORKS

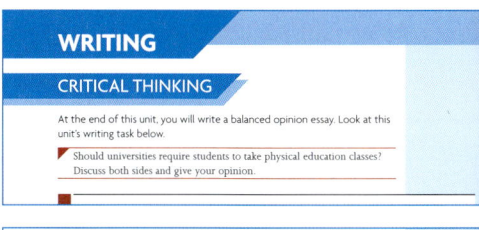

WRITING

Critical thinking
Develops the lower- and higher-order thinking skills required for the writing task.

Grammar for writing
Presents and practises grammatical structures and features needed for the writing task.

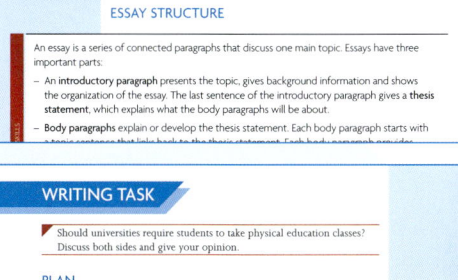

Academic writing skills
Practises all the writing skills needed for the writing task.

Writing task
Uses the skills and language learned throughout the unit to support students in drafting, producing and editing a piece of academic writing. This is the unit's main learning objective.

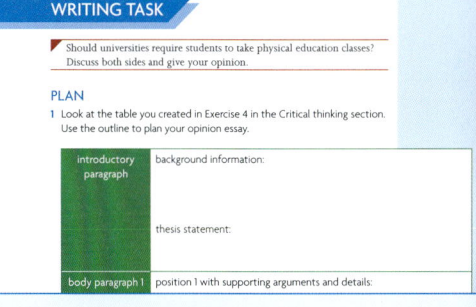

Objectives review
Allows students to evaluate how well they have mastered the skills covered in the unit.

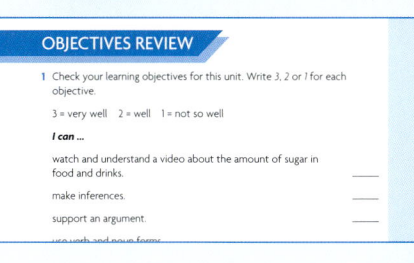

Wordlist
Lists the key vocabulary from the unit. The most frequent words used at this level in an academic context are highlighted.

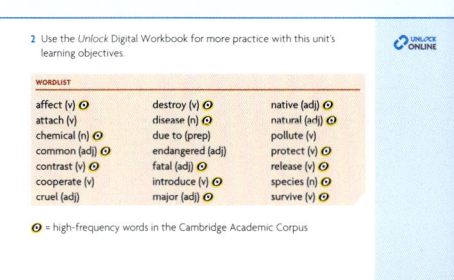

COMPONENTS

Unlock offers 56 hours per Student's Book, which is extendable to 90 hours with the Digital Pack, and other additional activities in the Teacher's Manual and Development Pack.

Unlock is a paired-skills course with two separate Student's Books per level. For levels 1–5 (CEFR A1 – C1), these are **Reading, Writing and Critical Thinking** and **Listening, Speaking and Critical Thinking**. They share the same unit topics so you have access to a wide range of material at each level. Each Student's Book provides access to the Digital Pack.

Unlock Basic has been developed for pre-A1 learners. **Unlock Basic Skills** integrates reading, writing, listening, speaking and critical thinking in one book to provide students with an effective and manageable learning experience. **Unlock Basic Literacy** develops and builds confidence in literacy. The *Basic* books also share the same unit topics and so can be used together or separately, and **Unlock Basic Literacy** can be used for self-study.

Student components

Resource	Description	Access

Student's Books	• Levels 1–5 come with the Digital Pack (Digital Workbook, Digital Classroom Material, downloadable audio and video)
	  – Levels 1–4 (8 units)
	  – Level 5 (10 units)
	• *Unlock Basic Skills* comes with downloadable audio and video (11 units)
	• *Unlock Basic Literacy* comes with downloadable audio (11 units)
		• The Digital Pack (Digital Workbook, Digital Classroom Material, downloadable audio and video) is accessed on our **learning platform** via the unique code inside the front cover of the Student's Book
		• The audio and video are downloadable from the Student's Resources section on the **learning platform**

Digital Workbook	• Levels 1–5 only • Extension activities to further practise the language and skills learned • All-new vocabulary activities in the Digital Workbook practise the target vocabulary in new contexts	• The Digital Workbook is on our **learning platform** and is accessed via the unique code inside the front cover of the Student's Book
Digital Classroom Material	• Levels 1–5 only • Extra practice in speaking, critical thinking and language	• Please go to **cambridgeone.org** to access the digital classroom material. • Students use the same login details as for the **learning platform**, and then they are logged in for a year
Video	• Levels 1–5 and *Unlock Basic Skills* only • All the video from the course	• The video is downloadable from the Student's Resources section on the **learning platform**
Audio	• All the audio from the course	• The audio is downloadable from the Student's Resources section on the **learning platform**

COMPONENTS

Teacher components

Resource	Description	Access
Teacher's Manual and Development Pack	• One manual covers Levels 1–5 • It contains flexible lesson plans, lesson objectives, additional activities and common learner errors as well as professional development for teachers, *Developing critical thinking skills in your students* • It comes with downloadable audio and video, vocabulary worksheets and peer-to-peer teacher training worksheets	• The audio, video and worksheets are downloadable from the Teacher Resources section on the **learning platform**
Presentation Plus	• Software for interactive whiteboards so you can present the pages of the Student's Books and easily play audio and video, and check answers	• Presentation Plus is available from the Teacher Resources section on our **learning platform**

LEARNING OBJECTIVES	IN THIS UNIT YOU WILL ...
Watch and listen	watch and understand a video about great egret and dolphin fishing teamwork.
Reading skill	read for main ideas in academic texts.
Critical thinking	compare and contrast facts.
Grammar	use comparative adjectives; use correct word order; combine sentences with *and*, *or*, *but*, *whereas*, *both*, *neither*.
Academic writing skill	write topic sentences.
Writing task	complete a comparison-and-contrast essay.

ANIMALS

UNIT 1

UNLOCK YOUR KNOWLEDGE

Work with a partner. Discuss the questions.

1 In your opinion, is it better to see animals in a zoo or in nature? Why?
2 Are there more wild animals in your country now, or were there more in the past? Why? Give examples.
3 Do humans need animals? Why / Why not?
4 Are animals important in your life? Why / Why not?

WATCH AND LISTEN

ACTIVATING YOUR KNOWLEDGE

PREDICTING CONTENT USING VISUALS

PREPARING TO WATCH

1 You are going to watch a video about dolphins and egrets. Before you watch, work with a partner and discuss the questions.

1 What do you know about dolphins? Where do they live and what do they eat?
2 What do birds eat? How do they get their food?

2 Work with a partner. Look at the photos from the video and discuss the questions.

1 Why and when might dolphins come onto land?
2 Why do you think dolphins live in groups, rather than alone?
3 What do the dolphins and the birds have in common?

GLOSSARY

marsh (n) an area of soft, wet land

egret (n) a large white bird with long legs which lives near water

surface (n) the top part or layer of something

mud bank (n) sloping raised land made of wet earth, especially along the sides of a river

shore (n) the land beside an ocean, a lake or a river

depend on (phr v) to need the help of someone or something in order to exist or continue as before

WHILE WATCHING

3 ▶ Watch the video. Number the sentences (a–e) in order (1–5).

a Young dolphins and egrets learn how to fish from their parents. _____
b Dolphins and egrets live together in the marshes of South Carolina. _____
c The dolphins' fishing is the only way some egrets get food. _____
d The egrets watch the dolphins in the water carefully. _____
e The dolphins push the fish onto land. _____

UNDERSTANDING MAIN IDEAS

4 ▶ Watch again. Write *T* (true), *F* (false) or *DNS* (does not say) next to the statements. Then, correct the false statements.

_____ 1 The egrets are experts on the dolphins' behaviour.
_____

_____ 2 The dolphins push the egrets onto the shore.
_____

_____ 3 When the fish are in the water, the dolphins start eating.
_____

_____ 4 The dolphins always use their left sides to push the fish.
_____

_____ 5 Some of the birds do not eat fish.
_____

UNDERSTANDING DETAIL

DISCUSSION

5 Work in small groups. Discuss the questions. Then, compare your answers with another group.

1 What other animals work together and help each other?
2 Why would two different animals work together?
3 What animals do humans work with? Why?

READING

READING 1

PREPARING TO READ

UNDERSTANDING KEY VOCABULARY

1 Read the definitions and complete the sentences with the correct form of the words in bold.

> **chemical** (n) a man-made or natural solid, liquid or gas made by changing atoms
> **destroy** (v) to damage something very badly; to cause it to not exist
> **due to** (prep) because of; as a result of
> **endangered** (adj) (of plants and animals) that may disappear soon
> **natural** (adj) as found in nature; not made or caused by people
> **pollute** (v) to make the air, water or land dirty and unhealthy
> **protect** (v) to keep something or someone safe from damage or injury
> **species** (n) a group of plants or animals which are the same in some way

1 The black rhino is one of the most _____ animals in the world. There are only about 5,000 left today.
2 There are three _____ of bears in North America. They are the American black bear, the grizzly bear and the polar bear.
3 Dangerous _____ from factories can kill fish and other animals when they enter lakes and rivers.
4 Smoke from factories can _____ the air and hurt both humans and animals.
5 When new homes are built, it often _____ the areas where animals live.
6 Few people visited the zoo last week _____ the cold weather.
7 I don't like zoos. I prefer to see animals in their _____ environments.
8 Many organizations are working to _____ endangered animals by creating safe places for them to live.

USING YOUR KNOWLEDGE

2 Look at the title and the first paragraph of the essay opposite and answer the question. What is the difference between an 'endangered' and an 'extinct' species? Then, complete the table with the names of any endangered and extinct species you know.

endangered species	extinct species

18 UNIT 1

3 Read the essay. Then, complete the table in Exercise 2 with the names of any other endangered animals mentioned in the essay.

Endangered species

1 An **endangered species** is a group of animals or plants which could soon become extinct. Extinction happens when the last animal of the species has died out and there will be no more. Many species are nearly extinct and could disappear from the Earth very soon if we don't do anything to save them. There are many reasons why species become endangered, but most harm to species is **due to** human activities such as habitat destruction, hunting and overfishing.

2 Habitat destruction is the main reason why animals become endangered. This happens in two ways. First, when humans move into a new area, they cut down trees to build houses and farms. This **destroys** the animals' habitat – the **natural** environment where plants or animals usually live – and leaves them without food. Animal habitats are also destroyed because of pollution. Dirty water from factories, which contains **chemicals**, ends up in rivers, and poisons used on farmland may even kill animals which live in the area.

3 Endangered species are also the result of hunting and fishing. Animals such as the Arabian oryx are nearly extinct because of the high price of their meat. Other animals are killed for their fur, bones or skin – or just for sport. For example, some seal species are now almost extinct because they are killed for their fur to make coats. Tigers are shot to make medicine and tea from their bones, and crocodiles are caught to make bags and shoes. Large sea creatures like whales, tuna and sharks have all become endangered species because of overfishing – too many are caught to make special dishes that people like to eat, such as shark's fin soup or sushi.

Arabian oryx

4 What steps can individuals and governments take to **protect** more animal and plant species from becoming endangered? We should try not to **pollute** natural areas, and farmers or companies who destroy animal habitats should face a financial penalty. The public can help out by refusing to buy products made from animals' body parts, such as seal fur coats or crocodile bags. Governments can help, too, by making it against the law to hunt, fish or trade in endangered species. They can also provide funding for animal sanctuaries and zoos. These protect animals from extinction by breeding more endangered animals, which can later be released into the wild. If we all cooperate by taking these steps, we will protect our planet so that our children and their children can enjoy it, too.

WHILE READING

> **Reading for main ideas in academic texts**
>
> In academic texts, you can find the main idea of a paragraph in the *topic sentence*, which is often the first sentence. It tells the most important thought or message of the paragraph. The middle sentences develop and support the main idea. The paragraph may have a *concluding sentence* with a summary or final comment.

READING FOR MAIN IDEAS

4 Read the essay again and write the paragraph number next to the main ideas.
   a How hunting and overfishing endanger animals ____
   b The definition of endangered and extinct species ____
   c How governments and citizens can protect animals ____
   d How humans destroy and pollute animal habitats ____

READING FOR DETAIL

5 Work with a partner. Answer the questions.
   1 According to the essay, what is the main cause of animal extinction and endangered species?
   _____
   2 How does pollution and cutting down trees cause problems for animals?
   _____
   3 What do people hunt animals for?
   _____
   4 Which large sea creatures are endangered because of overfishing?
   _____
   5 What can individuals do to protect animals from becoming endangered?
   _____
   6 What should governments do about the hunting and fishing of endangered animals?
   _____
   7 What should governments invest in to get more animals back into the wild?
   _____

READING BETWEEN THE LINES

WORKING OUT MEANING FROM CONTEXT

6 Read the last paragraph of the essay again and underline the words and phrases with the same meaning as the bold words.
   1 Companies who destroy animal habitats should **pay a fine**.
   2 You should help to protect animals by **choosing not to buy** fur.
   3 We can make it **illegal** to hunt, fish or trade in endangered species.
   4 Governments can **pay for** animal sanctuaries and zoos.
   5 If we **work together** by **taking these actions**, we can protect our planet.

DISCUSSION

7 Work with a partner. Discuss the questions.

1 What are some more examples of products which come from animals? Do you use any of these products?
2 Should governments spend money to save animal habitats even if this means there is less money for things people need, such as hospitals?

READING 2

PREPARING TO READ

1 Read the definitions and complete the sentences with the correct form of the words in bold.

> **common** (adj) happening often or existing in large numbers
> **cruel** (adj) causing pain or making someone or something suffer on purpose
> **disease** (n) illness; a serious health condition which requires care
> **fatal** (adj) causing death
> **introduce** (v) to put something into a place for the first time
> **major** (adj) most serious or important
> **native** (adj) used to describe animals and plants which grow naturally in a place
> **survive** (v) to stay alive; to continue to exist, especially after an injury or threat

1 Cats are very _____ in the streets of some Middle Eastern cities.
2 Plastic is often _____ to sea birds. Millions of birds die each year when they swallow plastic bags and other plastic waste.
3 The flu is a common _____ in humans, but some animals, such as horses, birds, seals and whales, can also get forms of the flu.
4 Many people believe that it is _____ to keep animals in zoos, where they can't move around freely.
5 Habitat loss is the _____ cause of species extinction in the Amazon River region.
6 Grey whales are endangered, but there is a chance that they will _____ because many countries have stopped hunting them.
7 There are many unique species which are _____ to the island of Madagascar, including more than 80 kinds of snakes.
8 Some animals become endangered when humans _____ new or foreign species into an area where they didn't exist before.

2 Work with a partner. Look at the photos in the article on page 23 and discuss the questions.

1 What are the animals in the photos? Do you have them in your country?
2 Which animal do you think is endangered? Why?

UNDERSTANDING KEY VOCABULARY

PREDICTING CONTENT USING VISUALS

READING FOR MAIN IDEAS

WHILE READING

3 Read the article and answer the questions.

1 What is an invasive species?

2 How did the grey squirrel enter the UK?

3 How are the two species of squirrels similar?

4 How are the two species of squirrels different?

5 What four reasons are given for the success of the grey squirrel in the UK?

SUMMARIZING

4 Read the summary and circle the correct words to complete it.

The article uses the example of the red and grey squirrel to explain what can happen when an invasive species competes with a native one. The (1)*grey / red* squirrel was introduced to the UK in the 19th century and has become very successful since then. Now there are (2)*fewer / more* than 140,000 native red squirrels left in the wild. The main reason why the grey squirrel is more successful is that it is (3)*fatter / thinner*, so it is less affected by cold weather. Another reason is that grey squirrels are (4)*unable / able* to live in cities. A further reason may be parapoxvirus, which (5)*kills / injures* red squirrels. Even though many people regard the grey squirrel as a (6)*pest / pet*, (7)*most / few* British people support destroying grey squirrels. Because red squirrels (8)*are / aren't* endangered worldwide, perhaps they could be reintroduced to Britain.

READING BETWEEN THE LINES

MAKING INFERENCES

5 Read the article again and answer the questions.

1 Paragraph 1 mentions one way that non-native species enter a new environment. What are some other ways?

2 Why do you think grey squirrels are regarded as 'major pests', apart from the damage they do to plants and houses?

3 What reason could some people give for trying to save the red squirrel?

4 Why do you think there are no grey squirrels on the Isle of Wight?

22 UNIT 1

Losing the battle for survival

1. Invasive species are plants and animals which arrive in an area where they are not **native**, usually due to human activity. For example, a species of shellfish might attach itself to the outside of a ship travelling between countries and enter a new environment in this way. Invasive species are often able to grow quickly in their new homes because they have no natural enemies. As a result, they may replace or damage native plants and animals which live in the same environment. One example is the case of grey and red squirrels in the UK.

2. Red squirrels used to be a **common** sight in British forests and countryside. Then, in the 1870s, the grey squirrel was **introduced** from North America because rich people thought the squirrels looked fashionable in the gardens of their large homes. Today, only about 140,000 red squirrels remain, mostly in Scotland. In contrast, grey squirrels are now extremely common and seen as **major** pests due to the damage they cause to plants and houses. While red squirrels are protected, grey squirrels can be legally trapped and destroyed.

3. At first sight, the two species of squirrel are similar. They both have a long tail, which helps them balance when jumping from tree to tree, and the same large eyes, small ears and powerful back legs.

4. In contrast, the two types of squirrel are different in body size and weight. The red squirrel has a typical head-and-body length of approximately 19 to 23 cm, a tail length of 15 to 20 cm and a body weight of 250 to 340 grams. The grey squirrel is larger than the red squirrel. The head and body measure between 23 and 30 cm, and the tail is between 19 and 25 cm long. Adult grey squirrels are also heavier, weighing between 400 and 600 grams. This size allows them to store more fat and helps them to **survive** hard winters, which could be **fatal** to their smaller cousins.

5. Three more differences explain why red squirrels have lost out in the competition with grey squirrels. First, red squirrels live high up in the trees, whereas grey squirrels spend more of their time on the ground. This means that any loss of forest habitat greatly affects the red squirrel population. Another reason is that grey squirrels are more intelligent and can adapt to new situations more easily than red squirrels. For example, they can survive in an urban environment because of their ability to use food provided by humans. A third problem for the red squirrel is **disease**. Both squirrels carry parapoxvirus. The virus does not seem to affect grey squirrels, but it is fatal to reds.

6. In conclusion, there does not seem to be much that scientists can do to help red squirrels survive in Britain. Some politicians support destroying populations of grey squirrels, but many British people would contend that this is **cruel**. Red squirrels have been successfully reintroduced from other countries, and they could be protected in places where there are no grey squirrels, such as the Isle of Wight. However, some people question whether Britain should protect red squirrels at all. Worldwide, they are not an endangered species. Considering the evidence, saving the red squirrel may be a waste of British government money. Government conservation funding should instead be spent on other endangered animals.

SYNTHESIZING

DISCUSSION

6 Work with a partner. Use ideas from Reading 1 and Reading 2 to answer the following questions.

1 Which reasons in Reading 1 and Reading 2 explain why the red squirrel is an endangered species?
2 Which of the solutions in paragraph 6 of Reading 2 do you think could help to save the red squirrel from extinction? Why?
3 In your opinion, is it important to try to save British red squirrels? Why / Why not?
4 Are introduced animal or plant species a problem in your country? Why? Give examples.

◉ LANGUAGE DEVELOPMENT

ACADEMIC VERBS

1 Read the sentences (1–6). Complete the definitions (a–f) with the words in bold.

1 Tigers are an endangered species. If people continue to hunt them, it will be impossible for them to **survive**.
2 Very cold and snowy winters **affect** some animals, such as rabbits and squirrels, since they are unable to find food as easily.
3 Seabirds are often hurt due to oil spills. When that happens, biologists catch the birds, clean them and then **release** them back to nature.
4 If we really want to save endangered species, governments and animal protection organizations need to **cooperate** and stop fighting each other.
5 Sometimes biologists catch endangered animals and **attach** a small radio to their bodies. Then, the biologists always know where the animals are.
6 In this paper, I intend to compare and **contrast** the appearance and behaviour of Indian and African elephants.

a _____ (v) to work together for a particular purpose
b _____ (v) to influence or cause something to change
c _____ (v) to allow someone or something to leave a place
d _____ (v) to stay alive; to continue to exist, especially after an injury or threat
e _____ (v) to show or explain differences between two people, situations or things
f _____ (v) to connect or join one thing to another

COMPARATIVE ADJECTIVES

Use the comparative form of an adjective + *than* to compare two people or things.

Add *-er* to one-syllable adjectives. If the adjective ends in *-e*, just add *-r*.	The red squirrel is **smaller than** the grey squirrel. The grey squirrel is **larger than** the red squirrel.
If the adjective ends in one vowel and one consonant (but not *w*), double the last consonant and add *-er*.	The grey squirrel is **bigger than** the red squirrel.
Use *more/less* + adjective + *than* for most adjectives with two or more syllables.	The grey squirrel is **more intelligent than** the red squirrel. The red squirrel is **less common than** the grey squirrel.
If an adjective with two syllables ends in *-y*, remove the *-y* and add *-ier*.	The grey squirrel is **heavier than** the red squirrel.

2 Complete the sentences using the comparative form with *than*.

1 The red squirrel is smaller and _____ (weak) the grey squirrel.
2 Grey squirrels are generally _____ (healthy) their smaller cousins because greys are not affected by parapoxvirus.
3 Grey squirrels are _____ (successful) red squirrels because they eat food provided by humans.
4 Red squirrels are _____ (endangered) grey squirrels, which are not at risk of extinction.

WRITING

CRITICAL THINKING

At the end of this unit, you will write two comparison paragraphs. Look at this unit's writing task below.

> Compare and contrast the two shark species in the diagram.

Comparing and contrasting facts

Graphic organizers can be useful for making notes on similarities and differences. One type of graphic organizer is a Venn diagram. Venn diagrams consist of two or more circles which overlap (cover part of the same space).

In Exercise 1 below, the Venn diagram shows the similarities and differences between red and grey squirrels. The characteristics only of red squirrels are listed on the left side of the diagram. The characteristics only of grey squirrels are listed on the right. The similarities between the two species are listed in the centre, where the circles overlap.

ANALYZE

1 Use your notes from Exercise 3 on page 22. Complete the Venn diagram with the similarities and differences between red and grey squirrels.

red squirrels
red in colour

both
live in Britain

grey squirrels
grey in colour

2 Work with a partner. Compare your answers and make any changes to your Venn diagram.

3 Look at the diagram of the two species of shark and read the information boxes in Exercise 4 below. Then, write a sentence for each feature to explain how the sharks are similar or different.

1 Size: _____
2 Colour: _____
3 Skin pattern: _____
4 Mouth: _____
5 Fins and tail: _____

4 Look at more information about the two sharks and answer the questions. Write W (whale shark) or T (tiger shark).

Whale shark
Animal class: Chondrichthyes (fish)
Habitat: Oceans
Length: 5.5–10 m
Weight: 18 tonnes
Colour: White stomach, grey-blue back and sides with light spots
Diet: Plankton, krill, other very small animals
Conservation status: Endangered (will probably become extinct)
Behaviour towards humans: No recorded attacks

Tiger shark
Animal class: Chondrichthyes (fish)
Habitat: Oceans
Length: 3.0–4.2 m
Weight: 0.86 tonnes
Colour: White stomach, grey-brown back and sides
Diet: Tuna, dolphins, turtles
Conservation status: Not currently at risk of extinction
Behaviour towards humans: Many reports of attacks on humans

1 Which shark is smaller? _____
2 Which shark is heavier? _____
3 Which shark eats large animals? _____
4 Which shark eats tiny sea creatures? _____
5 Which shark is in greater danger of extinction? _____
6 Which shark is more dangerous to humans? _____

APPLY

5 Look at the diagram and read the information boxes on the previous page again. Then, use your answers in Exercise 4 and the information about the whale shark and the tiger shark to complete the Venn diagram.

whale shark   both   tiger shark

GRAMMAR FOR WRITING

WORD ORDER

In English sentences, the subject usually comes before the verb and the object. These example sentences show some of the common features of English word order. Remember, they are not the only sentence structures in English.

subject	verb	object
Squirrels	eat	seeds, nuts and fruit.

subject	verb	adjective	prepositional phrase
Grey squirrels	are	common	in Britain.

linker	subject	verb	prepositional phrase
However,	they	were introduced	from North America.

linker	subject	verb	adjective
In addition,	they	have become	endangered.

1 Rewrite the words in the correct order.

1 lives / The tiger shark / in tropical oceans / .
   _____

2 isn't / the whale shark / However, / dangerous / .
   _____

3 The tiger shark / on its skin / markings / has / .
   _____

4 a large mouth / and / has / The whale shark / plankton / eats / .
   _____

COMBINING SENTENCES

> **and and or**
>
> When joining two sentences together, you can take out some words. For example, when the subject and verb are the same, you do not need to repeat them. When different adjectives describe the same noun, you do not need to repeat the noun. This makes the sentences shorter and better because you can avoid repetition.
>
> In affirmative sentences, use *and*:
> The tiger shark has sharp teeth. The tiger shark has a powerful bite.
> → The tiger shark has sharp teeth **and** a powerful bite.
>
> In negative sentences, use *or*:
> The tiger shark is not an endangered species. The tiger shark is not a protected species. → The tiger shark is not an endangered **or** (a) protected species.

2 Join the pairs of sentences with *and* or *or*. Take out the repeated words.

1 The whale shark is grey-blue. The whale shark has light spots on its body.
   _____ .

2 The tiger shark is grey-brown. The tiger shark has a striped pattern on its body.
   _____ .

3 The tiger shark eats large sea creatures. The tiger shark can be dangerous to humans.
   _____ .

4 The whale shark is not aggressive. The whale shark is not dangerous to swim with.
   _____ .

5 The whale shark is an endangered species. The whale shark is a protected species.
   _____ .

GRAMMAR

but and *whereas*

But and *whereas* are used to contrast two sentences. *Whereas* is more formal than *but*. Put a comma before *but* and *whereas*.

The tiger shark has sharp teeth and a powerful bite, **but/whereas** the whale shark does not have sharp teeth or a powerful bite.

3 Write three more sentences contrasting tiger sharks and whale sharks using *but* or *whereas*.

1 _____
_____ .
2 _____
_____ .
3 _____
_____ .

GRAMMAR

both and *neither*

You can use other phrases to compare two different things.

If two things/people have the same characteristic, use *both ... and ...* :
Both the grey **and** red squirrel carry parapoxvirus.
Both grey **and** red squirrels carry parapoxvirus.

If they do not have a particular characteristic, use *neither ... nor ...* :
Neither the grey **nor** the red squirrel has large ears.
Neither grey **nor** red squirrels have large ears.

Use a plural verb form with *both ... and*. Use a singular verb form for singular subjects and a plural verb form with plural subjects with *neither ... nor*.

4 Write sentences using the information in the table and *both ... and ...* or *neither ... nor ...* .

	red squirrels	grey squirrels
1 have long tails	yes	yes
2 live on the Isle of Man	no	no
3 are an endangered species	no	no
4 live in forests	yes	yes

1 _____ .
2 _____ .
3 _____ .
4 _____ .

ACADEMIC WRITING SKILLS

TOPIC SENTENCES

A **topic sentence** is usually the first sentence in a paragraph. It introduces the main idea of the paragraph, that is, the central point that the writer wants to make about the topic. It is a general statement about the paragraph's subject. It is then supported by the other sentences in the paragraph.

Look at three topic sentences from paragraphs in Reading 2. Notice that there are two types of topic sentences. The first type is a general statement of the topic. The second type also mentions the topics of the supporting sentences. Both kinds of topic sentence refer to the <u>main essay topic</u> (the situation of red squirrels and grey squirrels in Britain).

General statement
a At first sight, the two species of squirrel **are similar**.
b **Three more differences** explain why red squirrels have lost out in the competition with grey squirrels.

General statement + the topics of the supporting sentences
c In contrast, the two types of squirrel are different in **body size** and **weight**.

1 Look at the topic sentences (a–c) in the box above and at Reading 2 on page 23. Answer the questions.
   1 Which sentences above introduce paragraphs about differences? _____ _____
   2 Which sentence above introduces a paragraph about similarities? _____
   3 In Reading 2, how many supporting sentences does each paragraph have? Are all the paragraphs the same length? What does this tell you about the 'correct' number of sentences in a paragraph?
   _____
   _____
   _____

2 In the following two texts, the topic sentences are missing. Read each text and the three possible topic sentences (a–c) below it. Circle the letter of two possible topic sentences for each text.

1 Both bear species are native to North America and are common in both the United States and Canada. Neither the black bear nor the grizzly bear is an endangered species. Despite their names, the species are also similar in colour. 'Black' bears can be black, brown, red and even white. In the same way, grizzlies can range in colour from black to blond. Finally, the two bear species are similar in behaviour. They are intelligent, curious and gentle unless humans enter their area or try to hurt their babies. Then both bears can become dangerous.

   a Bears are one of the biggest attractions in the national parks of North America.
   b The American black bear and the grizzly, or brown, bear are similar in many ways.
   c The American black bear and the grizzly, or brown, bear are similar in habitat, colour and behaviour.

2 African elephants are much larger than Asian elephants and have much larger ears to protect them from the hot African sun. African elephants also have more wrinkled skin than their Asian cousins. Although the two species have tusks – large, curved teeth – only male Asian elephants have them, whereas both male and female African elephants do. However, despite these differences, the African and Asian species are similar in several important ways. First, both species are very social. They live in groups which are usually led by the oldest female. Second, elephants are naturally gentle animals. Neither African nor Asian elephants are dangerous to humans in normal circumstances.

   a African and Asian elephants are different in appearance, but they are similar socially.
   b African and Asian elephants have both differences and similarities.
   c African and Asian elephants are very similar in appearance.

WRITING TASK

Compare and contrast the two shark species in the diagram.

PLAN

1 Review your notes in the Venn diagram you created in Exercise 5 in the Critical thinking section.

WRITE A FIRST DRAFT

2 Read the introduction and the conclusion of the essay, which compares and contrasts the two shark species. Complete the essay by writing two paragraphs about the differences between the two species. Refer to the Task checklist on page 34.

The whale shark and the tiger shark

The whale shark and the tiger shark are two of the many shark species found in the major oceans of the world. Both the whale shark and the tiger shark belong to the animal class Chondrichthyes. Both types of shark have a large mouth, a divided tail and fins for swimming, including the large triangular fin which can often be seen above the surface of the water. On the other hand, these two types of shark are very different in their physical characteristics, diet, behaviour and conservation status.

_____
_____
_____
_____
_____
_____
_____
_____
_____
_____
_____
_____
_____
_____
_____
_____
_____
_____
_____

Overall, it is clear that the whale shark is a much larger animal, but it is a gentle giant, whereas the smaller tiger shark is a hungry meat-eater. However, both animals play an important role in the ocean environment. For example, tiger sharks keep the oceans clean by eating dead whales and fish. In my opinion, people and nations need to cooperate to make sure we protect both of these important animal species.

REVISE

3 Use the Task checklist to review your essay for content and structure.

TASK CHECKLIST	✔
Did you use a topic sentence to introduce each paragraph?	
Did you include information about the size, colour and weight of the two shark species?	
Did you include information about the diet, behaviour and conservation status of the two shark species?	

4 Make any necessary changes to your essay.

EDIT

5 Use the Language checklist to edit your essay for language errors.

LANGUAGE CHECKLIST	✔
Did you use academic verbs correctly?	
Did you use comparative adjectives correctly?	
Did you use *and*, *or*, *but*, *whereas*, *neither* and *both* correctly?	

6 Make any necessary changes to your essay.

OBJECTIVES REVIEW

1 Check your learning objectives for this unit. Write *3*, *2* or *1* for each objective.

3 = very well   2 = well   1 = not so well

I can ...

watch and understand a video about great egret and dolphin fishing teamwork.   _____

read for main ideas in academic texts.   _____

compare and contrast facts.   _____

use comparative adjectives.   _____

use correct word order.   _____

combine sentences with *and, or, but, whereas, both, neither*.   _____

write topic sentences.   _____

complete a comparison-and-contrast essay.   _____

2 Use the *Unlock* Digital Workbook for more practice with this unit's learning objectives.

WORDLIST

affect (v)	destroy (v)	native (adj)
attach (v)	disease (n)	natural (adj)
chemical (n)	due to (prep)	pollute (v)
common (adj)	endangered (adj)	protect (v)
contrast (v)	fatal (adj)	release (v)
cooperate (v)	introduce (v)	species (n)
cruel (adj)	major (adj)	survive (v)

◉ = high-frequency words in the Cambridge Academic Corpus

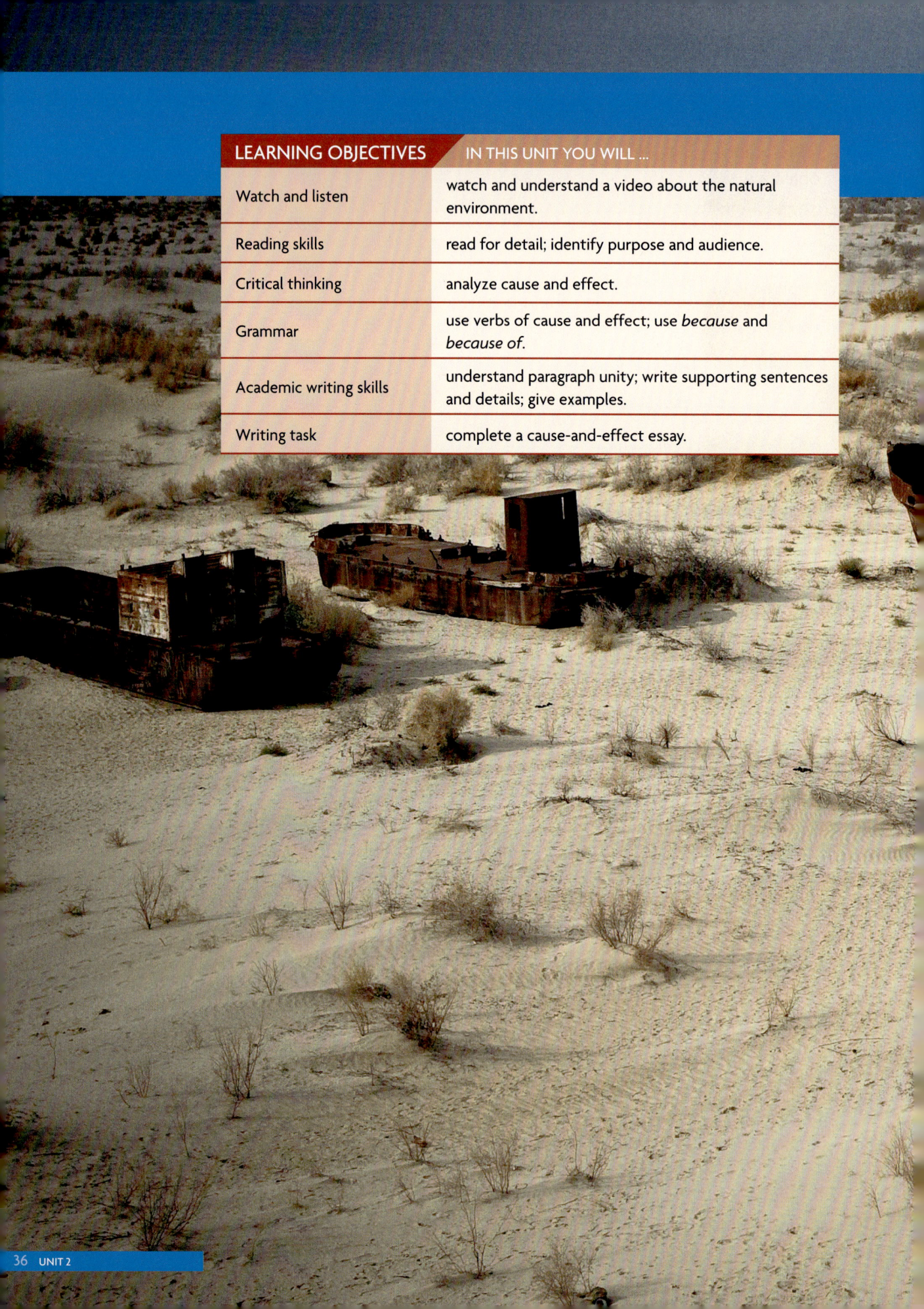

LEARNING OBJECTIVES	IN THIS UNIT YOU WILL ...
Watch and listen	watch and understand a video about the natural environment.
Reading skills	read for detail; identify purpose and audience.
Critical thinking	analyze cause and effect.
Grammar	use verbs of cause and effect; use *because* and *because of*.
Academic writing skills	understand paragraph unity; write supporting sentences and details; give examples.
Writing task	complete a cause-and-effect essay.

THE ENVIRONMENT

UNIT 2

UNLOCK YOUR KNOWLEDGE

Work with a partner. Discuss the questions.

1 Look at the photo. This was once one of the world's largest lakes. Where do you think it is? What might have caused it to dry up like this?
2 Is the weather changing in your country? How?
3 What are some ways that humans have affected the environment?
4 What is the biggest environmental problem in your country?

WATCH AND LISTEN

PREPARING TO WATCH

ACTIVATING YOUR KNOWLEDGE

1 You are going to watch a video about the natural environment. Before you watch, work with a partner and discuss the questions.

 1 Can you name any of the Seven Natural Wonders of the World?
 2 What are some important geographical features, like mountains or rivers, in your country?
 3 What street or place names in your city or country refer to geography? (e.g. Pacific Coast Highway, Lake Street)

PREDICTING CONTENT USING VISUALS

2 Work with a partner. Look at the photos from the video and discuss the questions.

 1 Where do you think these places are located – Europe, the USA or Japan?
 2 How old do you think these places are?
 3 What do you think formed these landscapes over time?

GLOSSARY

canyon (n) a deep valley with very steep sides

form (v) to create; to make something begin to exist or take a particular shape

cavern (n) a large cave

spectacular (adj) extremely good, exciting or beautiful

glacier (n) a large river of ice which moves very slowly, usually down a slope or valley

WHILE WATCHING

3 ▶ Watch the video. Number the sentences (a–f) in order (1–6).

> a The weather in the Grand Canyon can change very quickly. _____
> b Water is still changing the inside of Carlsbad Caverns. _____
> c Half Dome in Yosemite National Park was made by glaciers. _____
> d The Colorado River formed the Grand Canyon. _____
> e The rocks in the Grand Canyon are very old. _____
> f Yosemite Falls is the tallest waterfall in North America. _____

UNDERSTANDING MAIN IDEAS

4 ▶ Watch again. Circle the correct answer.

1 The Grand Canyon was formed in _____ years.
   a a million
   b a few million
   c a billion

2 Some of the rocks in the Grand Canyon are _____ the Earth.
   a as old as
   b half as old as
   c almost as old as

3 The weather in the Grand Canyon can suddenly change from _____ .
   a hot to dry
   b dry to wet
   c hot to cold

4 The Carlsbad Caverns is the _____ cave system in North America.
   a oldest
   b largest
   c widest

5 The water in Yosemite National Park comes from _____ .
   a snow
   b glaciers
   c a cave

UNDERSTANDING DETAIL

DISCUSSION

5 Work in small groups. Discuss the questions. Then, compare your answers with another group.

1 How might water change the Earth's geography in the next 100 years?
2 Do you think that glaciers will ever return to where you live?
3 Who should protect special natural areas in the world?

READING

READING 1

PREPARING TO READ

UNDERSTANDING KEY VOCABULARY

1 You are going to read an article about climate change. Before you read, look at the sentences (1–8) below and write the correct form of the words in bold next to the definitions (a–h).

1 The Amazon rainforest is one of the largest **ecosystems** in the world. It is home to more than 10% of all the known plants and animals on Earth.
2 Adelaide, Australia, has a very pleasant **climate**. The winters are not too cold and the summers are not too hot.
3 Pesticides – chemicals generally used to kill insects which damage plants – also **threaten** helpful insects, such as bees.
4 In order to fight pollution, scientists are developing car engines which use electric or solar energy instead of **fossil fuels** like gasoline.
5 Methane (CH_4) is a **greenhouse gas** which is found naturally inside the Earth and under the sea. It is used for cooking and heating homes and buildings.
6 The Earth's **atmosphere** is 480 km thick and contains a mixture of about 10 different gases, which we call *air*.
7 Because of **global warming**, polar ice is melting, sea levels are rising and some islands might soon be under water.
8 Habitat loss is the most important **cause** of species extinction.

a _____ (n) a gas which makes the air around the Earth warmer
b _____ (n) someone or something that makes something happen
c _____ (n) the layer of gases around the Earth
d _____ (n) the general weather conditions usually found in a particular place
e _____ (n) an increase in the Earth's temperature because of pollution
f _____ (v) to be likely to damage or harm something
g _____ (n) all the living things in an area and the effect they have on each other and the environment
h _____ (n) a source of energy like coal, gas and petroleum, that was formed inside the Earth millions of years ago

PREDICTING CONTENT USING VISUALS

2 Work with a partner. Look at the photo of the Upsala Glacier in Argentina on page 41 and discuss the questions.

1 What has happened to the glacier?
2 What do you think caused this change?
3 What are some other places where a similar change is happening today?
4 How do you predict this kind of change will affect the world?

OUR CHANGING PLANET

The Upsala Glacier in Argentina used to be one of the biggest glaciers in South America. In 1928, it was covered in ice and snow, but now the glacier is melting at an annual rate of about 200 m, so the area is covered in water. This is evidence of **global warming**.

1 In the last 100 years, the global temperature has gone up by around 0.75 °C. This may not sound like much, but such a small increase is causing sea levels to rise and **threatening** the habitat of many species of plants and animals. An increase of 2 °C in global temperatures could result in extinction for 30% of the world's land species.

2 The Northwest Passage is a sea route which runs along the northern coast of Canada between the Atlantic and Pacific Oceans. In the past, it was often difficult to use because the water was frozen; however, increasing temperatures and the subsequent deglaciation[1] have made it easier for ships to travel through this route. The trouble is that the melting of the ice is leading to loss of habitat for the polar bears and other species which live in this area.

3 Experts predict that global sea levels could rise by 30.5–122 cm by the end of the century. Consequently, some areas that were land a few hundred years ago are now under water, and many low-lying islands may be under water in the future.

4 As a result of the changing **climate**, the world's **ecosystems** are also changing faster than ever before. More than one-third of the world's mangrove forests[2] and around 20% of the world's coral reefs[3] have been destroyed in the last few decades. Forests are being cut down to provide land for food because human population is growing at such a rapid rate. Approximately a quarter of the land on Earth is now used for growing food. As a result of the higher temperatures and higher levels of carbon dioxide in the **atmosphere**, plants are producing more pollen, which could lead to more cases of asthma, a medical condition which makes it hard to breathe.

5 What is causing climate change? The main **cause** is the huge amount of **greenhouse gases**, such as methane and carbon dioxide (CO_2), in the atmosphere, but the reason for this is the world's population – you and me. As the population increases, more land is needed to provide food and energy. Burning **fossil fuels** for heating, lighting, transport, electricity or manufacturing produces CO_2. Furthermore, humans breathe out CO_2 while trees 'breathe in' CO_2 and produce oxygen, so by cutting down trees, we are increasing the amount of CO_2 in the atmosphere and reducing the amount of oxygen. As a result of human activities, CO_2 levels are now at their highest in 800,000 years.

6 The biggest challenge we all face is to prevent further environmental disasters. We must do something before it is too late. We need to reduce the amount of CO_2 in the atmosphere. We need to stop burning fossil fuels and start using renewable energy. We can get enough energy from renewable fuels, such as solar energy, hydroelectric energy or wind power, to be able to stop using fossil fuels completely.

[1]**deglaciation** (n) the melting of a glacier

[2]**mangrove forest** (n) large areas of trees and other plants which grow next to oceans, e.g. in Florida and Bangladesh

[3]**coral reefs** (n) colourful underwater ecosystems built by tiny animals

READING FOR MAIN IDEAS

SCANNING TO FIND INFORMATION

WHILE READING

3 Read the article and number the main ideas in the order which they appear.

solution to the problem _____
changing ecosystems _____
melting glaciers _____
causes of climate change _____

4 Read the article again. Then, complete the sentences using the words and phrases in the box.

> CO_2 levels   coral reefs   extinction   farming
> global temperatures   mangrove forests   sea levels

1 Over the last century, _____ have gone up by 0.75 °C.
2 Global increases in temperature could cause the _____ of 30% of land species.
3 _____ could rise by about 30.5 cm by the end of the century.
4 Recently, over a third of the world's _____ have been destroyed.
5 Twenty percent of the Earth's _____ have been lost in the last few decades.
6 Twenty-five percent of the land on Earth is used for _____ .
7 _____ are at their highest for 800,000 years.

Reading for detail

In a paragraph, the sentences which come after the topic sentence contain *supporting details* – information to help the reader understand the main idea more fully. Types of supporting details include facts, statistics, examples, reasons, explanations, comparisons and descriptions.

Often, the topic sentence includes words which tell you what type of supporting sentences to expect in the body of the paragraph. For example:

Topic sentence: What is causing climate change?

The words *is causing* tell you that the paragraph will use causes, or reasons, to explain the main idea.

5 Read the article again and complete the table with supporting details.

READING FOR DETAIL

1 country where the Upsala Glacier is located	
2 name of sea route through the Arctic ice	
3 why forests are being cut down all over the world	
4 medical problem caused by pollen	
5 main chemicals responsible for climate change	
6 human activities that reduce the amount of oxygen in the atmosphere	
7 what we should do to reduce the amount of CO_2 in the atmosphere	

READING BETWEEN THE LINES

Identifying purpose and audience

It is useful to think about an author's purpose – what the author was trying to do when writing a text – as well as the audience, or intended reader(s) of a text. This information can give you an idea about the organization of a text and its function.

SKILLS

6 Work with a partner. Discuss the questions.

1 What was the author's main purpose in writing this article?
   a to inform the reader about the causes and effects of global warming
   b to describe changes in mangrove forests and coral reefs
   c to persuade people to help reduce CO_2 levels by using renewable energy
2 Who is the intended audience for this article?
   a advanced science students
   b general adult readers
   c university professors

IDENTIFYING PURPOSE AND AUDIENCE

7 What information in the article helped you choose your answer?

DISCUSSION

8 Work with a partner. Discuss the questions.

1 Are there any advantages to the melting of the glaciers in the Northwest Passage? Give reasons for your answer.
2 What are some possible disadvantages of using renewable energy like solar energy or wind power?

READING 1   43

READING 2

PREPARING TO READ

PREVIEWING

1 You are going to read an essay about deforestation. Before you read, look at the photo and the title of the essay on page 45. Then, answer the questions.

1 Why are trees important for the environment?
_____
_____

2 Why do people cut down trees?
_____
_____

3 What will happen if we destroy too many trees?
_____
_____

UNDERSTANDING KEY VOCABULARY

2 Read the definitions and complete the sentences with the correct form of the words in bold.

> **absorb** (v) to take in a liquid or gas through a surface and hold it
> **construction** (n) the process of building something, usually large structures such as houses, roads or bridges
> **destruction** (n) the act of causing so much damage to something that it stops existing because it cannot be repaired
> **effect** (n) result; a change which happens because of a cause
> **farming** (n) the job of working on a farm or organizing work on a farm
> **logging** (n) the activity or business of cutting down trees for wood
> **rainforest** (n) a forest in a tropical area with a rainfall of 250 cm or more per year

1 Clothes made from plants, like cotton or bamboo, _____ water more easily than man-made materials like polyester.
2 _____ has been my family's occupation since my grandfather bought his first cow 75 years ago.
3 _____ hurts native people because it destroys the forest that provides them with food, shelter and medicine.
4 The Amazon _____ in South America receives 200 to 600 cm of rain every year.
5 Because of heavy snow, the _____ of the new road stopped for more than two months.
6 Sunburn is just one of the harmful _____ of too much sun on sensitive skin.
7 In 2017, Hurricane Harvey caused serious _____ in the US state of Texas and killed more than 80 people.

44 UNIT 2

THE CAUSES AND EFFECTS OF DEFORESTATION

1 Forests, which cover almost one-third of the surface of the Earth, produce oxygen and provide homes to plants, animals and humans. These days, many of the world's great forests are threatened by *deforestation* – the process of removing trees from large areas of land. The **destruction** of forests occurs for several reasons; trees are used as fuel or for **construction**, and cleared land is used as pasture[1] for animals or fields for planting food. The main harmful **effects** of deforestation are climate change and damage to animal habitats.

2 The main causes of deforestation are commercial **farming** by big business and farming by local people. Huge commercial farms have taken over large areas of forest in many countries. In Indonesia, for example, industrial **logging** is carried out to clear huge areas for the production of palm oil, while in Brazil, large areas of the Amazon **rainforest** are cleared to grow soy and vegetable oil. In contrast, local farmers may cut down and burn trees to clear an area just big enough to graze cattle or grow crops. However, after two or three years, the land can no longer be used, so the farmer moves to another piece of land. Normally, it takes around ten years for cleared land to recover, but in populated areas the land is never allowed to recover. This constant reuse of land leads to heavy erosion[2] – the loss of the top layer of soil which protects the ground. Erosion, in turn, can cause flooding in heavy rain.

3 One serious effect of deforestation is climate change. Normally tropical rainforests help control the Earth's temperature by **absorbing** carbon dioxide. As an example, the vast rainforest of the Amazon covers an area around 25 times the size of the UK and absorbs an estimated 1.36 billion tonnes of carbon dioxide annually. However, in areas where deforestation has taken place, the carbon dioxide goes into the atmosphere and traps heat in a process called the *greenhouse effect*. The result is global warming. Increasing global temperatures result in less rain. This causes the rainforests to dry out and leads to fires – which cause more emissions of carbon dioxide. In this way, the rainforests actually contribute to global warming instead of helping to solve it.

4 Forest destruction also has an effect on biodiversity[3]. Deforestation causes the loss of habitats and damage to land where plants and animal species live, leading to the extinction of many species. A decrease in biodiversity threatens entire ecosystems and destroys future sources of food and medicine.

5 In conclusion, damage to the world's forests is leading to changes in the natural environment and causing global warming. Looking to the future, governments should act to plant more trees which will absorb carbon dioxide and protect forests from illegal logging. Otherwise, deforestation on such a large scale is sure to have terrible effects on the environment.

[1] **pasture** (n) an area of land with grass for animals to eat
[2] **erosion** (n) the gradual damage or removal of stone, soil, etc. by wind, rain or waves
[3] **biodiversity** (n) the variety of different animals and plants in an area

WHILE READING

SUMMARIZING

3 Read the essay and complete the summary using the words in the box.

> animals   crops   decade   deforestation   effects
> environment   erosion   habitats   protected   warming

The essay discusses the human causes of (1)_____ and the (2)_____ on the environment. Trees are removed for grazing of (3)_____ and growing (4)_____ like soy and palm oil. Farmers traditionally leave the land for a (5)_____ before reusing it, but if the land is constantly reused, it results in (6)_____ of the soil. Deforestation allows CO_2 to escape into the atmosphere and contributes to global (7)_____ . It also affects biodiversity because it leads to the loss of (8)_____ . Governments should make sure forests are (9)_____ from logging. Otherwise, deforestation will have terrible consequences for the (10)_____ .

READING FOR DETAIL

4 Read the essay again and correct the factual mistakes in the sentences.

1 In Indonesia, trees are cut down to make way for olive oil plantations.
   _____

2 Farmers can graze animals on their land for ten years.
   _____

3 The rainforests of the Amazon cover an area 2.5 times the size of the UK.
   _____

4 Deforestation protects future sources of food and medicine.
   _____

5 Governments should plant more trees to absorb oxygen.
   _____

6 Small-scale deforestation will have disastrous effects on the environment.
   _____

READING BETWEEN THE LINES

MAKING INFERENCES

5 Work with a partner. Answer the questions.

1 What does the writer mean by the phrases *industrial logging* and *commercial farming*?
   _____

2 What will probably happen if the Amazon rainforest disappears?
   _____

3 Why does deforestation reduce future sources of food and medicine?
   _____

DISCUSSION

6 Work with a partner. Use ideas from Reading 1 and Reading 2 to answer the following questions.

1 As the world's climate changes, which places will have too much water? Which places will become drier? Give examples.
2 How do both the melting of the glaciers and deforestation cause the extinction of species?

SYNTHESIZING

LANGUAGE DEVELOPMENT

ACADEMIC VOCABULARY

1 Replace the underlined words in the sentences with the academic words in the box.

> annual (adj)   areas (n)   challenge (n)   consequences (n)
> contributes to (phr v)   issue (n)   predict (v)   trend (n)

1 The most serious <u>problem</u> which threatens the environment is climate change. _____
2 Experts <u>think</u> that there will not be enough fresh water in the future. _____
3 Pollution and climate change are the <u>results</u> of human activity. _____
4 Fortunately, we are seeing a <u>pattern</u> where people recycle more and use less packaging. _____
5 In some <u>places</u>, the glaciers have melted or even disappeared as a result of higher temperatures. _____
6 The <u>yearly</u> rate of species loss in the rainforest is nearly 50,000 – that's 135 plant, animal and insect species each day! _____
7 The biggest <u>test</u> we face is to protect the planet. _____
8 Human activity <u>causes</u> climate change. _____

ENVIRONMENT COLLOCATIONS

2 Match the words in each box to make collocations about the environment. Sometimes more than one collocation is possible.

> carbon   climate
> environmental   greenhouse
> natural   power   tropical

> change   dioxide   gas
> group   plant   rainforest
> resource

3 Complete the sentences with the correct form of the collocations from Exercise 2.

1 In my town, about 70% of the electricity comes from a _____ which uses coal for energy.
2 Carbon dioxide and methane are examples of _____ .
3 Almost all scientists these days agree that _____ is happening and is a serious threat to our planet.
4 Trees absorb _____ and give off oxygen.
5 All over the world, _____ are working to educate people about the dangers of deforestation and habitat destruction.
6 Fresh water is the most precious _____ on Earth.
7 Thousands of unique plants, animals, birds and insects live in the _____ of South America and Southeast Asia.

48 UNIT 2

WRITING

CRITICAL THINKING

At the end of this unit, you will write two paragraphs of a cause-and-effect essay. Look at this unit's writing task below.

> Describe the human causes of climate change and the effects that climate change will have on the planet.

Analyzing cause and effect

Cause and effect is a very common type of academic writing. Sometimes the causes and effects are discussed in separate paragraphs. This is true especially when there is one cause with several effects or one effect with several causes. For example:

Problem: traffic congestion in my city
Cause: too many cars on the road
Effects: air pollution; noise; people are often late to work or school; accidents

However, causes and effects are often connected in a chain of events. When describing a cause-and-effect chain, it is useful to write about several causes and several effects in the same paragraph. For example:

Problem: traffic congestion in my city
Cause 1: a shortage of housing → **Effect 1**: people live in the suburbs
Cause 2: people live in the suburbs → **Effect 2**: they must drive to get to work

1 Work in small groups. Look back at Reading 2 and complete the table of causes and effects.

DEFORESTATION

CAUSES	EFFECTS
commercial farming by big business	

UNDERSTAND

2 Read paragraph 3 of Reading 2 again. Complete the cause-and-effect chain with the numbers of the items (1–6) from the box.

| 1 less rain | 2 more CO$_2$ emissions | 3 fires |
| 4 global warming | 5 forests dry out | 6 CO$_2$ enters atmosphere and traps heat (greenhouse effect) |

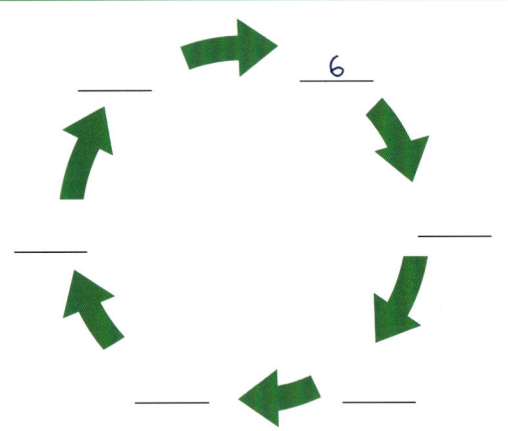

___ → _6_
↑   ↓
___   ___
↑   ↓
___ ← ___

REMEMBER

APPLY

3 Using information from Reading 1 and Reading 2 as well as your own ideas, brainstorm the human causes and effects of climate change.

4 Use your answers from Exercise 3 to create a cause-and-effect chain diagram. Then compare diagrams with a partner.

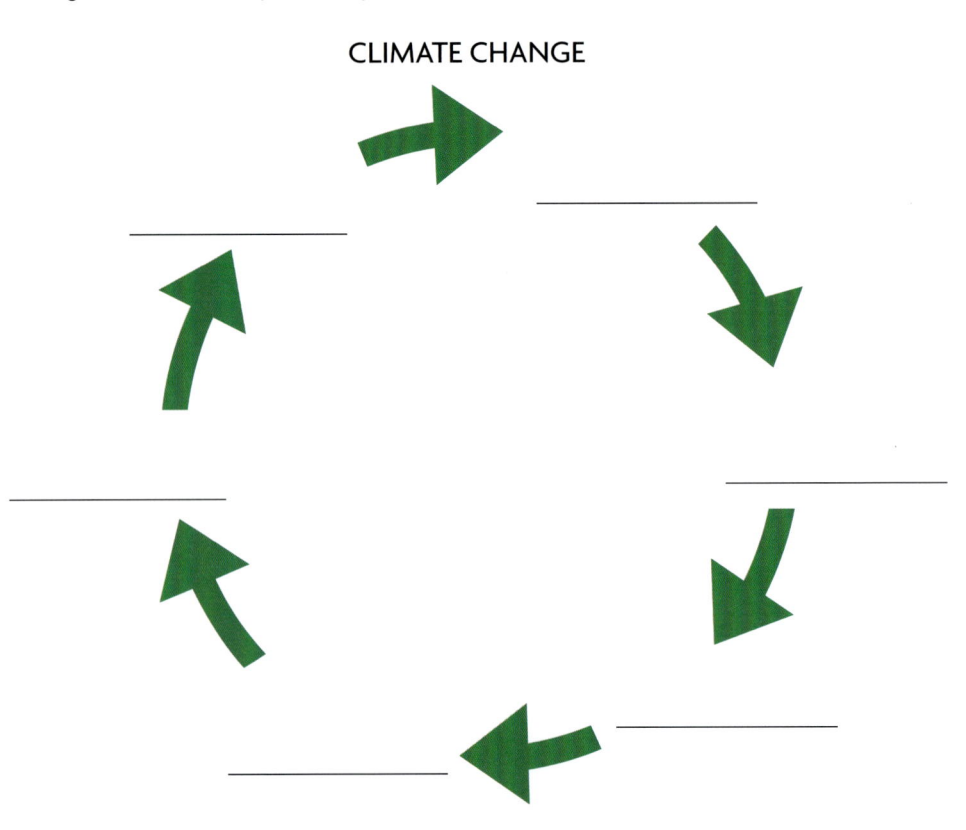

CLIMATE CHANGE

___ → ___
↑   ↓
___   ___
↑   ↓
___ ← ___

GRAMMAR FOR WRITING

VERBS OF CAUSE AND EFFECT

Writers use certain phrases to show the relationship between the causes of a problem and its effects. Look at the sentences below.

cause	linking verb or phrase	effect
Deforestation	leads to causes results in	habitat destruction.

effect	linking verb or phrase	cause
Habitat destruction is	caused by due to the result of	deforestation.

1 Complete the table by adding linking cause-and-effect verbs or phrases. More than one answer is possible. The first one has been done for you as an example.

Global warming ⁽¹⁾ _leads to_ higher temperatures and ⁽²⁾_____ melting glaciers.	Melting glaciers are ⁽³⁾_____ higher temperatures, which are ⁽⁴⁾_____ global warming.

2 Complete the sentences using one linking word or phrase.
  1 Deforestation _____ in animal extinction and loss of biodiversity.
  2 Demand for food and energy are expected to rise _____ to the increase in the world's population.
  3 Burning fossil fuels _____ an increase in CO_2 in the atmosphere.
  4 Flooding, heat waves and other extreme weather are all _____ by climate change.
  5 Reducing the amount of meat we eat may _____ in lower greenhouse gas emissions.
  6 Submerged islands could be the _____ of rising sea levels.

BECAUSE AND BECAUSE OF

> **GRAMMAR**
>
> *Because* is a conjunction which introduces a reason. It is followed by a subject, a verb and sometimes an object.
>
> The environment is changing **because** humans are burning fossil fuels.
>
> *Because of* is a two-word preposition meaning 'as a result of'. It is followed by a noun, a pronoun or a noun phrase.
>
> The climate is changing **because of** human activity.

3 Complete the sentences using *because* or *because of*.
  1 Sea levels may rise _____ melting glaciers.
  2 In a warmer world, there are more fires _____ there is less rain.
  3 The atmosphere is becoming warmer _____ deforestation and burning fossil fuels.
  4 Low-lying islands may be submerged _____ sea levels are rising.

ACADEMIC WRITING SKILLS

PARAGRAPH UNITY

> **SKILLS**
>
> A well-written paragraph has just one main idea, and all the supporting sentences in the paragraph should explain or give information about it. They should not introduce any new topics.
>
> When a paragraph has these characteristics, it has **unity**. Unity is a basic requirement of good academic writing.

1 In the paragraph, circle the main idea. Then, cross out one sentence which does not support that idea.

Bottled water
Do you drink water from plastic bottles? If you do, you might want to think about changing your habit, because plastic water bottles hurt both people and the environment. First of all, plastic bottles contain two harmful chemicals: BPA and phthalates. Both types of chemicals can cause serious health problems in both adults and children. Second, plastic bottles hurt the environment. The bottles are made from petroleum, and transporting them requires an enormous amount of polluting fossil fuels. In the 1970s, the United States was the world's biggest exporter of fossil fuels. Also, most plastic bottles are not recycled. They end up in our landfills, where they can take many decades to break down. Because of these harmful effects of plastic water bottles on people and the environment, I have stopped buying them. I now drink water from the tap, and guess what: it tastes good!

SUPPORTING SENTENCES AND DETAILS

Good writers use **supporting sentences** to develop and explain the main idea of a paragraph. The supporting sentences state important points about the main idea. Normally, writers provide **details** – facts, examples, reasons or explanations – for each supporting point in a paragraph.

Look at the outline of a paragraph from Reading 2. Notice the kinds of details it includes.

Topic sentence: The main causes of deforestation are commercial farming by big business and farming by local people.

1st supporting sentence: Huge commercial farms have taken over large areas of forest in many countries.

Details (examples): In Indonesia, for example, industrial logging is carried out to clear huge areas for the production of palm oil, while in Brazil, large areas of the Amazon rainforest are cleared to grow soy and vegetable oil.

2nd supporting sentence: In contrast, local farmers may cut down and burn trees to clear an area just big enough to graze cattle or grow crops.

Details (facts/explanation): However, after two or three years, the land can no longer be used, so the farmer moves to another piece of land. Normally, it takes around ten years for cleared land to recover, but in populated areas, the land is never allowed to recover.

Details (reasons): This constant reuse of land leads to heavy erosion – the loss of the top layer of soil which protects the ground. Erosion, in turn, can cause flooding in heavy rain.

2 Read the paragraph *Bottled water* on the opposite page again and answer the questions.

1 Find two supporting sentences and underline them.
2 What detail is given to explain the first supporting sentence? Is this a fact, example or reason?
   _____

3 How do plastic bottles harm the environment, according to the paragraph? What details does the paragraph include to explain each effect – facts, examples or reasons?
   _____
   _____
   _____

Giving examples

Examples are a common type of supporting detail. Look again at this extract from Reading 2.

*Huge commercial farms have taken over large areas of forest in many countries. In Indonesia, **for example**, industrial logging is carried out to clear huge areas for the production of palm oil.*

The first sentence makes it clear that there are 'many countries' in which commercial farms have taken over large areas of forest. In the second sentence, the writer states Indonesia as an example of this. The example provides specific detail to make the point more effectively.

Good writers use a range of expressions to introduce examples.

especially	like	such as
including	for example	One (Another) example is ...
particularly	for instance	One (Another) suggestion / method / idea is ...

3 Complete the sentences below using the words and phrases in the box.

> Africa, Asia and the Middle East   climate change
> lakes   northern Lebanon   peas and beans
> placing stones   trees   the Gobi Desert

Desertification is a process in which land becomes drier, losing bodies of water **such as** (1)_____ as well as wildlife and vegetation, **particularly** (2)_____ . Desertification has a number of causes, **including** (3)_____ , deforestation and damaging farming methods.

Desertification is a very serious problem in many regions of the Earth, **especially** poor parts of (4)_____ . **For instance,** (5)_____ in China is the fastest-growing desert in the world. Photos from space have shown sand dunes forming less than 45 km from Beijing! **Another example is** (6)_____ , where forests were destroyed in order to build cities.

Desertification is a serious global problem, but now local people are trying solutions to reduce or prevent it where they live. Farmers in some dry areas plant *leguminous* plants **like** (7)_____ , which pull nitrogen from the air and make the soil richer. **Another method is** (8)_____ around the base of trees. The rocks provide shade for the roots and help trees and insects survive. But the best solution of all is planting trees, or just not cutting them down in the first place.

WRITING TASK

Describe the human causes of climate change and the effects that climate change will have on the planet.

PLAN

1 Look at the cause-and-effect chain you created in Exercise 4 in the Critical thinking section.

2 Look at the structure of the essay on page 45 as you plan your own essay.

3 Refer to the Task checklist on page 56 as you prepare your paragraphs.

WRITE A FIRST DRAFT

4 Read the introduction and conclusion of the cause-and-effect essay below. Complete the introduction paragraph by writing two or three causes of climate change that you will discuss in your body paragraphs.

5 Then, complete the essay by writing two body paragraphs: one about the human causes of climate change and another about the effects. Remember to list the two or three causes you mentioned in the introduction.

Causes and effects of climate change

Introduction: The Earth's climate has changed several times throughout history. According to the National Aeronautics and Space Administration (NASA), there have been seven cycles of warming and cooling in the last 650,000 years. These earlier cycles occurred naturally as a result of changes in the atmosphere. In contrast, nearly all climate scientists agree that the climate changes we are seeing today are caused by human activities, especially _____ , and these activities are having serious negative effects on our planet.

Conclusion: To conclude, human activity is clearly causing the climate to change and, as a result, the planet is experiencing a number of negative effects. It is important that we reduce our negative impact on the planet as much as possible – for example, by using renewable energy instead of fossil fuels – before it is too late.

REVISE

6 Use the Task checklist to review your essay for content and structure. If you have any problems with content, look back at the Critical thinking section.

TASK CHECKLIST	✔
Did you include two or three causes and effects from your notes in the Critical thinking section?	
Did you use a suitable topic sentence for each paragraph?	
Does each paragraph include supporting sentences?	
Does each paragraph have unity?	
Did you include facts, examples or reasons to explain each supporting sentence?	

7 Make any necessary changes to your essay.

EDIT

8 Use the Language checklist to edit your essay for language errors.

LANGUAGE CHECKLIST	✔
Did you use the correct collocations for the environment?	
Did you use verbs of cause and effect correctly?	
Did you use *because* and *because of* correctly?	
Did you use the correct tenses, nouns and adjectives?	

9 Make any necessary changes to your essay.

OBJECTIVES REVIEW

1 Check your learning objectives for this unit. Write *3, 2* or *1* for each objective.

3 = very well   2 = well   1 = not so well

I can …

watch and understand a video about the natural environment.   _____

read for detail.   _____

identify purpose and audience.   _____

analyze cause and effect.   _____

use verbs of cause and effect.   _____

use *because* and *because of*.   _____

understand paragraph unity.   _____

write supporting sentences and details.   _____

give examples.   _____

complete a cause-and-effect essay.   _____

2 Use the *Unlock* Digital Workbook for more practice with this unit's learning objectives.

WORDLIST

absorb (v)	construction (n) ⊙	greenhouse gas (n)
annual (adj) ⊙	contribute to (phr v)	issue (n) ⊙
area (n) ⊙	destruction (n) ⊙	logging (n)
atmosphere (n) ⊙	ecosystem (n)	predict (v) ⊙
cause (n) ⊙	effect (n) ⊙	rainforest (n)
challenge (n) ⊙	farming (n) ⊙	threaten (v)
climate (n) ⊙	fossil fuel (n)	trend (n) ⊙
consequences (n) ⊙	global warming (n)	

⊙ = high-frequency words in the Cambridge Academic Corpus

LEARNING OBJECTIVES	IN THIS UNIT YOU WILL ...
Watch and listen	watch and understand a video about the jumbo jet.
Reading skill	predict content using visuals.
Critical thinking	evaluate solutions to a problem.
Grammar	make suggestions; use the first conditional; use *if ... not* and *unless*.
Academic writing skill	write a concluding sentence.
Writing task	complete a problem–solution essay.

TRANSPORT

UNIT 3

UNLOCK YOUR KNOWLEDGE

Work with a partner. Look at the photo.
1 How many different types of transport can you name?
2 Which modes of transport do you use? Answer the questions.
  1 Why do you use these modes of transport?
  2 Why do you not use the other modes of transport?

WATCH AND LISTEN

PREPARING TO WATCH

ACTIVATING YOUR KNOWLEDGE

1 You are going to watch a video about planes. Before you watch, work with a partner and discuss the questions.

1. What is the biggest plane you have ever been on?
2. What is the longest flight you have ever taken?
3. How many hours do you think a plane can fly without stopping?

PREDICTING CONTENT USING VISUALS

2 Work with a partner. Look at the photos from the video and discuss the questions.

1. How old do you think this plane is?
2. Who would use the room in the third photo?
3. What are the differences between first class and economy class on planes today?

GLOSSARY

jumbo jet (n) a very large plane which can carry hundreds of passengers
straight (adv) following one after the other without stopping
lounge (n) a room in a hotel, theatre, airport, etc. where people can relax or wait

WHILE WATCHING

UNDERSTANDING MAIN IDEAS

3 ▶ Watch the video. Complete the summary with the words in the box.

| changed | flew | had | helped | worked |

In 1969, the 747 [1]_____ across the Atlantic Ocean. Jimmy Barber [2]_____ build the first 747. He and his team [3]_____ for many hours a day to complete it. The first 747 [4]_____ two floors, with a lounge on the second floor. The 747 [5]_____ air travel forever.

60 UNIT 3

4 Watch again. Circle the correct answer.

UNDERSTANDING DETAIL

1 The ability to carry more _____ changed air travel.
   a fuel   **b** people   **c** baggage

2 Today, many planes can travel for _____ hours without stopping.
   a 20   **b** 18   **c** 14

3 In 1969, the 747 was the most _____ plane in the world.
   a modern   **b** expensive   **c** famous

4 The first 747s could carry about _____ people.
   a 500   **b** 747   **c** 1,000

5 The _____ of air travel today is much lower than it was 50 years ago.
   a cost   **b** speed   **c** comfort

DISCUSSION

5 Work in small groups. Discuss the questions.

1 What are the advantages of air travel?
2 What are the disadvantages of air travel?

6 Complete the table with one advantage and one disadvantage for each kind of transport with your group. Then, compare your answers with another group.

transport	advantage	disadvantage
1 car		
2 train		
3 bus		
4 bicycle		
5 boat		

READING

READING 1

PREPARING TO READ

Predicting content using visuals

The images which accompany a text can provide valuable information about the content. For example, they can tell you where the text is set, what it is about, what kind of text it is (essay, blog post, etc.), what the key points are and much more. All this information helps you make predictions about what you are going to read, and once you start reading, it helps you focus on the important information in the reading.

PREDICTING CONTENT USING VISUALS

1 Work with a partner. You are going to read a news article about a new kind of city. Before you read, look at the photos of transport in two cities and answer the questions.

1 What problem can you see in the first photo? Does your city have this problem?

2 What is the vehicle in the second photo? How could it be a solution to the problem in Question 1? Where do you think the photo was taken?

3 How is transport in the two photos different?

2 Read the definitions and complete the sentences with the correct form of the words in bold.

> **commuter** (n) someone who travels between home and work or university regularly
> **connect** (v) to join two things or places together
> **destination** (n) the place where someone or something is going
> **outskirts** (n) the outer area of a city or town
> **public transport** (n) a system of vehicles, such as buses and trains, which operate at regular times for public use
> **rail** (n) the form of transport which uses trains
> **traffic congestion** (n) when too many vehicles use a road network and it results in slower speeds or no movement at all

1 Vancouver, British Columbia, has an outstanding system of _____ , so it isn't necessary to own a car there.
2 I like living on the _____ of the city because there is more open space and the air is cleaner.
3 I take the train to work every day because the _____ network is fast and cheap.
4 _____ has improved since my city built a metro and improved the bus system. Fewer people drive to work now.
5 I told the bus driver that my _____ was the city centre, so she told me to get off on Main Street.
6 In large cities, people usually prefer to live near their workplace so that they don't have to be a _____ , but it's more expensive than the suburbs.
7 Ferries _____ the mainland to the islands.

WHILE READING

3 Read the news article on page 64 and answer the questions.
1 Which features are designed to make Masdar City cooler than the area around it?

2 What is a PRT, and how does it work?

3 Apart from the PRT, what other transport options are available in Masdar City?

4 How did the financial crisis of 2008–2009 affect Masdar City?

UNDERSTANDING KEY VOCABULARY

READING FOR MAIN IDEAS

Masdar: City of the future

1 Abu Dhabi, the capital of the United Arab Emirates, is a modern city with a population of about 1.8 million people. The expanding economy and rising population have brought great benefits to Abu Dhabi, but with them have come a major problem: traffic jams. Abu Dhabi, like many cities in the United Arab Emirates, suffers from **traffic congestion**. The average commuting time of 45 minutes is fairly high.

2 One answer to the congestion problem is Masdar City. Masdar is a new city of 6 km² being built on the **outskirts** of Abu Dhabi. The city combines traditional Arabic architecture with energy efficiency. For example, Masdar gets all of its electricity from solar power. There is a wall around the city to keep out the hot desert wind and the streets are narrow, to provide shade from the sun and allow a breeze to pass through. As a result, the city is about 10 °C cooler than in Abu Dhabi.

3 There is no traffic congestion in Masdar because cars are not allowed. Instead, people use **public transport**. An underground **rail** system and a light-rail transit system run through the centre of the town and **connect** Masdar to Abu Dhabi and the airport. A unique transport system called Personal Rapid Transit (PRT) was also planned and partially built. The original plan was to have 3,000 solar-powered, driverless 'podcars' which could carry passengers to about 100 stations all around the city. The vehicles would also be used to transport **commuters** from stations on the outskirts of the city, where they would leave their own cars, to their **destinations** in the city. In reality, only 13 PRTs are in operation today, because developments in technology have made it easier and cheaper to operate electric vehicles. Today, PRTs are used to carry passengers from the outskirts to the Masdar Institute of Science and Technology in the centre. At the same time, Masdar residents can use clean-energy electric cars and buses to travel around the city.

4 Masdar City was originally projected to cost around $24 billion, but the global financial crisis of 2008–2009 reduced the amount of money which was available for the project. A few people worried that Masdar could become a 'green ghost town' – a place in which nobody would want to live. Yet today, construction is continuing, and Masdar City is expected to be completed sometime before 2030. When it is finally finished, there could be as many as 50,000 residents and 40,000 daily commuters. As work on the city continues and international businesses such as Siemens choose to locate offices there, city planners are confident that Masdar's green solutions to both traffic and environmental problems will outweigh the financial cost of building the city.

4 Read the article again. Complete the sentences using a number or no more than three words.

1 Abu Dhabi has a big problem with _____ .
2 The average time it takes to get to work is _____ .
3 Masdar's electricity comes from _____ .
4 Traffic jams are not a problem in Masdar because cars are _____ in the city.
5 Originally, Masdar City was supposed to cost $ _____ .
6 In the future, _____ people could live in Masdar, with _____ travelling into the city for work each day.

READING FOR DETAIL

READING BETWEEN THE LINES

5 Work with a partner. Read the article again and answer the questions.

1 What are the possible benefits of Abu Dhabi's expanding economy and rising population?
_____
_____

2 Masdar will be a small city with several advantages. What will be some disadvantages of living there?
_____
_____

3 Do you think the planners of Masdar City will decide to expand the PRT system in the future? Why / Why not?
_____
_____

MAKING INFERENCES

DISCUSSION

6 Work with a partner. Discuss the questions.

1 Would you like to live in Masdar City? Why / Why not?
2 Do you agree that the benefits of Masdar City will outweigh the financial cost of building it? Why / Why not?
3 Would a PRT system work in your city? Why / Why not?

READING 2

PREPARING TO READ

UNDERSTANDING KEY VOCABULARY

1 Read the definitions and complete the sentences with the correct form of the words in bold.

> **cycle** (v) to travel by bicycle
> **emergency** (n) an unexpected situation which requires immediate action
> **engineering** (n) the activity of designing and building things like bridges, roads, machines, etc.
> **fuel** (n) a substance like gas or coal which produces energy when it is burned
> **government** (n) the group of people that controls a country or city and makes decisions about laws, taxes, education, etc.
> **practical** (adj) useful; suitable for the situation it is being used for
> **vehicle** (n) any machine which travels on roads, such as cars, buses, etc.

1 I don't own a car, but I have a bicycle. I usually _____ to work if the weather is nice.
2 If I want to use public transport, I need to take three buses to get to school. This isn't _____ , so I usually drive my car.
3 A Boeing 747 jet burns about 11 tonnes of _____ an hour in flight. That's equal to about 3.8 litres each second.
4 The _____ wants people to drive less, so it passed a law which requires drivers to pay a high tax on petrol.
5 The 166-km Danyang–Kunshan Grand Bridge in China is an incredible work of _____ .
6 In Masdar, drivers must park their _____ outside the city and use public transport to reach the city centre.
7 In my apartment I have a first-aid kit, a fire extinguisher and a torch in case of an _____ .

PREDICTING CONTENT USING VISUALS

2 Work with a partner. You are going to read an essay about solving traffic congestion. Before you read, look at the photos on page 67 and answer the questions.

1 What solutions to the problem of traffic congestion do the photos show?
   _____

2 What other solutions to traffic congestion do you think the article will discuss?
   _____
   _____

1. Traffic congestion is a serious problem in cities worldwide. There are simply too many **vehicles** competing for too little space. The company TomTom, which does research on traffic in cities worldwide, estimated that in 2015 the average commuter wasted 100 hours during the evening rush hour alone. In addition to wasting people's time, traffic jams have many other negative effects. Therefore, **governments** everywhere are working hard to find solutions to this problem.

2. Traffic jams have negative effects on drivers, cities and the environment. To begin with, they cause stress to drivers, which may lead to health problems or road rage[1]. Traffic jams can also lead to economic losses because products cannot be delivered on time, and employees arrive late for work or meetings. Another negative effect is that **emergency** services can become caught in traffic and are, therefore, unable to get to an emergency in time. Finally, traffic congestion negatively affects the environment. Traffic congestion wastes **fuel**, which in turn produces more carbon dioxide through car exhaust[2] and contributes to the greenhouse effect. Taken together, all these effects have a serious negative impact on the quality of people's lives.

3. Because of these serious effects, it is important for cities and governments everywhere to take steps to reduce road congestion. The most obvious solutions involve **engineering**. This means building more roads with wider lanes so that more cars can travel at the same time, as well as constructing tunnels and bridges to guide drivers around congested areas. However, the costs for engineering solutions are extremely high. Another problem is that more roads may actually result in more traffic. In short, engineering solutions have both advantages and disadvantages.

4. Other, more creative, solutions to the congestion problem are to increase the tax on fuel or to make people pay to travel in the centre of a city or on a motorway. If governments increase the cost of driving, people will think more carefully about using their cars. However, taxing fuel and roads may mean that some people cannot afford to drive their cars, and they may have to give up their jobs. Also, governments may not want to increase the fuel tax too much if the tax is unpopular with voters.

5. A more popular solution, therefore, would be to promote other forms of transport, like ferries, cycling and underground trains. One suggestion is to encourage people to **cycle** more. Although cycling has obvious health benefits and does not pollute the air, it is not **practical** in every climate and can prove dangerous in heavy traffic.

6. Another possibility is to persuade people to use buses, although they are inconvenient for some people. A related option is a park-and-ride system which allows people to drive to the outskirts of cities, park, and then take a bus to the city centre. This allows some flexibility for car drivers and reduces congestion in the centre of the city. A disadvantage for people who work late shifts[3] is that many buses do not run at night.

7. Overall, cities are using a variety of methods to tackle the problem of traffic congestion. Most of the methods have advantages as well as disadvantages. We should encourage alternative forms of transport because they reduce the amount of traffic on the roads and also have a positive effect on the environment.

[1]**road rage** (n) violence committed by angry drivers in traffic
[2]**exhaust** (n) smoke that comes out of a car as a result of burning petrol
[3]**late shifts** (n) work hours that are late in the day or at night

WHILE READING

READING FOR MAIN IDEAS

3 Read the essay and circle the best title.

a The effects of traffic congestion in cities
b Solving the problem of traffic congestion
c Urban traffic congestion is increasing
d Bicycles can solve urban traffic congestion

READING FOR DETAIL

4 Read the essay again. What are the four negative effects of traffic congestion mentioned in the essay? Write your answers.

_____ _____
_____ _____

5 Read the essay again. Complete the table of solutions to the problem of traffic congestion. Write one word in each blank. In some items, more than one answer is possible.

	solutions	advantages	disadvantages
engineering	Build more roads, (1)_____ and bridges.	More vehicles can (2)_____ at once.	This may (3)_____ in more traffic.
tax	Increase tax on roads and (4)_____.	People will think more about using their cars.	Some people may need to give up their (5)_____.
cycling	Encourage people to cycle more.	It has benefits for your (6)_____ and reduces pollution.	It can be dangerous when (7)_____ is heavy.
park-and-ride	People park and then travel into the city centre by (8)_____.	It reduces (9)_____ in the city centre.	Buses may not operate at (10)_____.

6 Work with a partner. Compare your answers to Exercises 3–5. Make any necessary changes.

READING BETWEEN THE LINES

MAKING INFERENCES

7 Work with a partner. Answer the questions.

1 What sort of health problems might be caused by stress?
_____

2 Why would a person in the government not want to have an unpopular tax?
_____

3 Why are buses inconvenient for some people?
_____

DISCUSSION

8 Work with a partner. Use ideas from Reading 1 and Reading 2 to answer the following questions.

1 Are Abu Dhabi's traffic problems similar to the problems in other big cities? Give an example.
2 Review the solutions for reducing traffic congestion in Masdar City. Could these solutions work in other big cities? Why / Why not?
3 In addition to the solutions suggested in Reading 1 and Reading 2, can you think of other solutions to traffic congestion?

SYNTHESIZING

LANGUAGE DEVELOPMENT

TRANSPORT COLLOCATIONS

1 Match the words to make collocations about transport. Sometimes more than one collocation is possible.

1 traffic
2 public
3 cycle
4 rush
5 car
6 road
7 parking

a transport
b restrictions
c congestion
d lane
e share
f rage
g hour

2 Complete the sentences with collocations from Exercise 1.

1 _____ is usually from eight to nine in the morning, and then again from four in the afternoon to seven in the evening.
2 I use _____ like trains or the underground to get to work.
3 If people get angry and behave aggressively in traffic, they are expressing _____ .
4 Because of _____ , you can't leave your car there.
5 _____ is a big problem in this city. The traffic jams are terrible.
6 I am in a _____ and drive to work with a colleague.
7 You can't drive in the _____ . It's only for bicycles.

SYNONYMS FOR VERBS

Synonyms are words which have the same, or very similar, meaning. Use synonyms in your writing to avoid repetition.

New roads will **stop** traffic congestion in the short term. The local government hopes this will **prevent** delays.

3 Rewrite the sentences using the verbs from the box to replace their synonyms in bold.

| attempt | consider | convince | produce | reduce | require | waste |

1 We **need** more public transport in the city, like a light-rail network.
_____

2 Commuters **try** to arrive on time, but traffic often causes delays.
_____

3 Masdar City uses solar energy to **make** its electricity.
_____

4 It's important for people in industrial countries to **lower** their use of energy.
_____

5 Traffic congestion causes people to **use** time and energy **in an inefficient way**.
_____

6 We should **think about** cycling instead of using our cars to travel short distances.
_____

7 It will be difficult to **get** drivers to use public transport.
_____

MAKING SUGGESTIONS

When you write an academic essay, you may need to make suggestions. You can use *should* to do this. However, when you make more than one suggestion and you want to avoid repetition, use other ways to say *should*.

Look at the sentences below. They show different expressions for making a suggestion in an academic essay.

Cities **should encourage** commuters to use public transport.
It is important to encourage commuters to use public transport.
Encouraging commuters to use public transport **is a good idea**.

Notice how you need to add *-ing* to a verb (*encouraging*) when you use it as a noun. This is a good way to make an action the subject of your sentence.

4 Look at the suggestions with *should* and complete the sentences so that the meaning is the same.

We should use bicycles to travel short distances.
1 It is important to _____ .
2 _____ is a good idea.

We should build more high-speed railways between cities.
3 It is important to _____ .
4 _____ is a good idea.

We should consider new ways of reducing traffic congestion.
5 It is important to _____ .
6 _____ is a good idea.

5 Complete the sentences using the phrases in the box.

> is a good idea   it is important   we should

1 There are a number of reasons why _____ use public transport instead of driving.
2 Another reason why using public transport _____ is that it reduces the amount of pollution from cars.
3 It seems to me that _____ encourage people to use cycle lanes more by building more and making them safer.
4 _____ for people of all ages to be able to use public transport.
5 I am not entirely convinced that _____ use public transport for all local journeys instead of driving.
6 Some people doubt whether spending money to build an underground rail system _____ .

WRITING

CRITICAL THINKING

At the end of this unit, you will write two paragraphs about possible solutions to a problem. Look at this unit's writing task below.

▌ Discuss the advantages and disadvantages of two solutions to a city's traffic congestion problems.

SKILLS

Evaluating solutions to a problem

Sometimes there is more than one solution to a problem. When that is the case, you should evaluate each of the different solutions and decide which is the best. To do this, you will need to consider the points for and against each solution. For this topic, these might include how cheap, fast, convenient or popular it is.

UNDERSTAND

1 Work with a partner. Look back at Reading 2. Then, choose three of the possible solutions which are mentioned and complete the table.

problem	goal(s)
Traffic congestion	

solutions	advantages/disadvantages
	+
	−
	+
	−
	+
	−

decisions(s)	reason(s)

2 Study the map of Riverton and list the city's potential traffic problems.

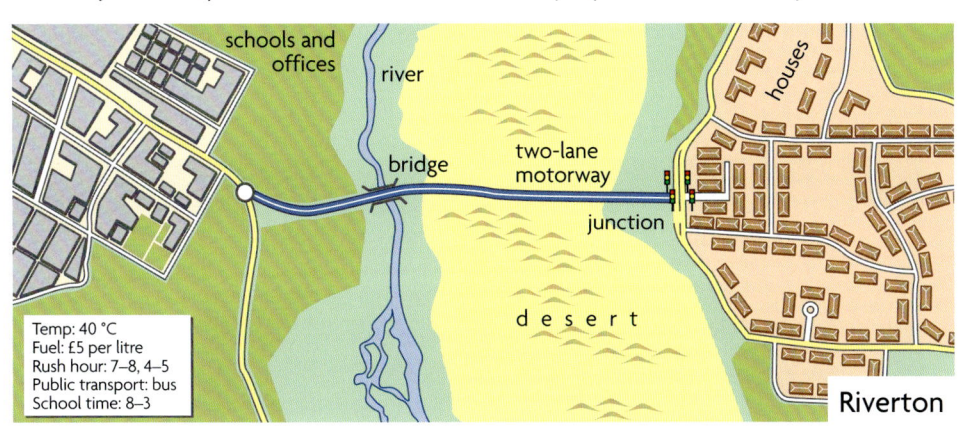

schools and offices
river
bridge
two-lane motorway
junction
houses
desert
Riverton

Temp: 40 °C
Fuel: £5 per litre
Rush hour: 7–8, 4–5
Public transport: bus
School time: 8–3

> The area where people live is on one side of the bridge, and the business centre and schools are on the other side.

3 Complete the first two boxes of the table with the main problem and goals for solving the problem.

problem	goal(s)

solutions	advantages/disadvantages
	+
	−
	+
	−
	+
	−

decisions(s)	reason(s)

EVALUATE

4 Look at the map on the previous page again and the possible solutions to the traffic problem below. What are the advantages and disadvantages of each solution? Choose three solutions and write their advantages and disadvantages in the table on the previous page.

build a tunnel	encourage people to cycle
cost: £3 million	cost: £500,000
time to implement: 2 years	time to implement: 3 months
park-and-ride bus system	move the residential area to the other side of the river
cost: £2 million	cost: £100 million
time to implement: 1 year	time to implement: 10 years
road tax	ferry
cost: £100,000	cost: £2.5 million
time to implement: 3 months	time to implement: 2 years

5 Look at the four solutions and choose the best two. Write them in the decision(s) box and write your reasons in the reason(s) box on the previous page.

6 Compare your decision(s) with a partner. Do you agree? If not, why not?

GRAMMAR FOR WRITING

FIRST CONDITIONAL

You can use *first conditionals* to persuade or negotiate. Notice the use of *if* and *will* to combine two sentences.

idea/action: The council creates a park-and-ride scheme.

consequence: The city can reduce pollution.

If the council creates a park-and-ride scheme, the city **will be able to** reduce pollution. The city **will be able to** reduce pollution **if** the council creates a park-and-ride scheme.

Notice:
- The idea/action clause begins with *if*.
- The consequence clause uses *will*.
- *Can* changes to *be able to* in the consequence clause.
- Either the idea clause or the consequence clause can come first. If the idea clause comes first, put a comma after it.

1 Join the pairs of sentences using *if* and *will*. Remember to change *can* to *be able to* in Question 5. More than one answer is possible.

1 We move the offices and schools next to the houses. We have fewer traffic problems.
_____

2 We have a ferry over the river. Fewer people use the bridge.
_____

3 Fewer cars use the roads. We increase the price of fuel.
_____

4 We change the office hours. The cars won't all use the road at the same time.
_____

5 We build a railway line. People can use the train instead of their cars.
_____

IF ... NOT AND *UNLESS*

> **GRAMMAR**
>
> You can also use *if ... not* or *unless* to describe the consequence of not doing a certain action.
>
> **idea/action**: The council creates a park-and-ride scheme.
>
> **consequence**: The city can reduce pollution.
>
> **If** the council **doesn't** create a park-and-ride scheme, the city **won't be able to** reduce pollution.
>
> The city **won't be able to** reduce pollution **unless** the council creates a park-and-ride scheme.

2 Join the sentences using *if ... not* or *unless*. Remember to use a negative verb in the consequence clause.

1 The traffic will improve. We build more roads. (if not)
   The traffic won't improve if we don't build more roads.

2 Pollution will be reduced. We use cleaner transport. (unless)
_____

3 We provide a solution. People will get to work on time. (if not)
_____

4 We will solve the traffic problem. We build houses closer to the business areas. (unless)
_____

5 The city invests in public transport. There will be less congestion. (if not)
_____

ACADEMIC WRITING SKILLS

WRITING A CONCLUDING SENTENCE

Some paragraphs have a concluding sentence. Usually, this sentence reminds the reader of the topic sentence. It can do this by restating the main idea, but with different words. It can also summarize the main points of the paragraph. Writers often add a concluding comment, such as their opinion or a prediction. Compare these topic and concluding sentences:

Topic sentence: Since 2006, Masdar City has run into serious financial difficulties.

Concluding sentence: If all goes well, Masdar's green solutions to both traffic and environmental problems will outweigh the financial cost of building the city.

1 Read the paragraphs. Then, circle the best concluding sentence (a–c) for each one.

Paragraph 1
Cycling to work has both advantages and disadvantages. The most important advantage is that it saves me time because I don't have to wait in traffic or spend time searching for a parking space. Cycling is great exercise, and it feels good. Also, cycling helps the environment because it does not create any pollution. However, there are two things I dislike about cycling. One is that it can be dangerous if drivers can't see you. Also, some drivers are very rude.

a In other words, some drivers think they own the road and cyclists have no place on it.
b Still, I think the advantages of cycling outweigh the disadvantages, and I will continue to use my bicycle to get around in good weather.
c Because of these disadvantages, I may sell my bicycle and take the bus.

Paragraph 2
In some cities, such as Seattle and Istanbul, people commute to work by ferry. A ferry carries people, and sometimes cars, over water between two or more places. Sometimes a ferry is the only way to get around because there are no roads or bridges. However, even if a road exists, many people prefer to travel by ferry because it saves time. Ferry passengers don't have to sit in traffic, and they can read or work on their computers. Another benefit is that ferries help the environment by keeping hundreds of cars and lorries off the roads.

a These advantages explain why people in cities all over the world travel to and from work by ferry.
b For me, the best thing about taking the ferry to work is that it is fun.
c Many ferries have a restaurant on board, and passengers can drink coffee or eat a meal while they commute.

WRITING TASK

> Discuss the advantages and disadvantages of two solutions to a city's traffic congestion problems.

PLAN

1 Look at the table you created in Exercise 3 in the Critical thinking section and complete the outline.

Solution 1: _____
Advantages: _____
_____
Disadvantages: _____
_____

Solution 2: _____
Advantages: _____
_____
Disadvantages: _____
_____

2 Review the Task checklist on page 78 as you prepare your paragraphs.

WRITE A FIRST DRAFT

3 Read the introduction and conclusion to the essay and complete the essay by writing about the advantages and disadvantages of two solutions to Riverton's traffic problems. Then, write a concluding sentence for each paragraph.

Solving Riverton's traffic congestion problem

Introduction: Riverton's unusual geography causes it to have bad traffic congestion. People have to travel from their homes on one side of the river and desert to their offices and schools on the other. Unfortunately, there is only one main road running through the city centre and just one bridge which connects the residential and business areas. Moreover, the only public transport is a bus which uses the same road. There is also a junction near the housing area where the traffic builds up during the two rush hours, when people commute to work or drop off their children at school. After a long period of study, we have proposed two possible solutions to the traffic problems in Riverton. Both solutions have advantages and disadvantages.

> **Conclusion:** In conclusion, of the many solutions which we have considered, these two had the most advantages. Although these plans are not perfect, there is no doubt that they will help reduce the traffic congestion in Riverton. This will have benefits both for people's health and for the environment. The people of Riverton should support these solutions.

REVISE

4 Use the Task checklist to review your essay for content and structure. If you have any problems with content, look back at the Critical thinking section.

TASK CHECKLIST	✔
Did you write two solution paragraphs in the main body? Do the topic sentences state the solutions?	
Did you explain the advantages and disadvantages of each solution?	
Did you write a concluding sentence for each paragraph?	

5 Make any necessary changes to your essay.

EDIT

6 Use the Language checklist to edit your essay for language errors.

LANGUAGE CHECKLIST	✔
Did you use transport collocations correctly?	
Did you use synonyms for verbs to make your writing more interesting and academic?	
Did you use correct language for making suggestions?	
Did you use first conditionals correctly?	
Did you use *if*, *will*, *if ... not* and *unless* correctly?	

7 Make any necessary changes to your essay.

OBJECTIVES REVIEW

1 Check your learning objectives for this unit. Write *3*, *2* or *1* for each objective.

3 = very well   2 = well   1 = not so well

I can ...

watch and understand a video about the jumbo jet.   _____

predict content using visuals.   _____

evaluate solutions to a problem.   _____

make suggestions.   _____

use the first conditional.   _____

use *if ... not* and *unless*.   _____

write a concluding sentence.   _____

complete a problem–solution essay.   _____

2 Use the *Unlock* Digital Workbook for more practice with this unit's learning objectives.

WORDLIST

attempt (v)	engineering (n)	rail (n)
commuter (n)	fuel (n)	reduce (v)
connect (v)	government (n)	require (v)
consider (v)	outskirts (n)	traffic congestion (n)
convince (v)	practical (adj)	vehicle (n)
cycle (v)	prevent (v)	waste (v)
destination (n)	produce (v)	
emergency (n)	public transport (n)	

◉ = high-frequency words in the Cambridge Academic Corpus

LEARNING OBJECTIVES	IN THIS UNIT YOU WILL …
Watch and listen	watch and understand a video about the Coming of Age Day in South Korea.
Reading skills	annotate a text; preview a text.
Critical thinking	respond to an author's ideas.
Grammar	avoid generalizations; use adverbs of frequency to avoid generalizations; paraphrase.
Academic writing skill	write a summary and a personal response.
Writing task	write a summary paragraph and a response paragraph.

CUSTOMS AND TRADITIONS

UNIT 4

UNLOCK YOUR KNOWLEDGE

Work in a small group. Discuss the questions.

1 Look at the photo. Where do you think it was taken? What is happening?
2 Are there any customs or traditions connected with food in your country? What are they?
3 What is the future for traditions like this? Can they be saved or will they be lost? Why?

WATCH AND LISTEN

PREPARING TO WATCH

ACTIVATING YOUR KNOWLEDGE

1 Work with a partner. You are going to watch a video about a coming-of-age celebration in South Korea. Answer questions 1–3 about each action in the box. Then discuss question 4.

> buy a house   drive a car   get married
> own a credit card   ride a motorcycle

1 At what age are people in your country allowed to do each of these things?
2 Why do you think this age was chosen?
3 Do you think the age should be older or younger? Why / Why not?
4 What do you think *coming of age* means? At what age does it happen in your country?

PREDICTING CONTENT USING VISUALS

2 Work with your partner. Look at the photos and tick the activities you think you will see in the video.

☐ giving presents
☐ wearing traditional clothes
☐ making a speech
☐ taking part in a ceremony
☐ learning something new
☐ eating particular foods
☐ taking photos

GLOSSARY

rights (n pl) things the law allows you to do

responsibility (n) something that you must look after, deal with, pay for, etc.

date back (phr v) to have existed for a particular length of time, or since a particular time

formal (adj) (of language, clothes and behaviour) suitable for serious or important occasions

ritual (n) a set of particular actions, and sometimes words, which are part of a ceremony belonging to a particular culture

WHILE WATCHING

UNDERSTANDING MAIN IDEAS

3 ▶ Watch the video and check your ideas in Exercise 2. Then work in pairs and discuss the question.

What are the differences between the modern and the traditional celebrations of coming-of-age day in South Korea?

UNDERSTANDING DETAIL

4 ▶ Watch again. Complete the sentences about the coming-of-age day celebration in South Korea.
1 South Korean 19-year-olds celebrate becoming adults on the same _____ .
2 They often receive _____ roses as a gift – one for each year of their lives.
3 The gift of perfume has a special _____ .
4 The hair-changing ceremony is over _____ years old.
5 _____ wear a **jade** hairpin and a **crown** with many **ornaments**.
6 Young men use a _____ to put their hair in a **topknot**.
7 Young men wear a _____ made of **bamboo** and horsehair.
8 They learn how to put on *hanbok,* which are traditional, _____ clothes.
9 The young people **bow** to their _____ .
10 Parents tell their adult children how _____ they are.

WORKING OUT MEANING FROM CONTEXT

5 Complete the definitions with the correct form of the words in bold in Exercise 4.
1 _____ an object that is beautiful rather than useful
2 _____ to bend your head or body forward to show respect
3 _____ a tall, hard grass found in hot countries, which is used to make many products
4 _____ a circle-shaped decoration for the head, often made of gold and jewels
5 _____ an expensive green stone from which jewellery is made
6 _____ long hair tied up high on the head

DISCUSSION

6 Work in small groups. Choose a traditional celebration in your country. Then discuss the questions.
1 What traditions of this event have stayed the same? Why?
2 How has the modern celebration changed? Do you think these changes are a good or a bad thing? Why?

READING

READING 1

PREPARING TO READ

UNDERSTANDING KEY VOCABULARY

1 You are going to read an article about customs and traditions in different countries. Before you read the article, read the definitions below. Complete the sentences with the correct form of the words in bold.

> **appearance** (n) the way someone or something looks
> **culture** (n) the way of life, especially customs and beliefs, of a group of people
> **exchange** (v) to give something to someone and receive something that they give you
> **expect** (v) to think that something will or should happen
> **formal** (adj) (of clothes, behaviour or language) serious or very polite
> **greet** (v) to welcome someone with particular words or actions
> **relationship** (n) the way two people or groups feel and behave towards each other

1 I love travelling because I enjoy experiencing other _____ and their food, celebrations and traditions.
2 In Japan, it is customary for business people to _____ business cards when they meet for the first time.
3 In Korea and some Spanish-speaking countries, people do not _____ a woman to change her last name when she gets married.
4 In Thailand, people _____ each other by holding their hands together, bowing and saying 'Sawadee', which is similar to 'Hello' or 'Good day' in English.
5 Many languages have two ways to say *you*. They have a _____ word to use in polite situations like work and a different word for family and friends.
6 I always spend a lot of time on my hair and clothes before a special occasion. I want to make sure my _____ is perfect.
7 In most cultures, people who have a close family _____ enjoy spending time together and giving each other gifts.

2 What 'rules' do visitors to your country need to know in order to be polite? Write notes in the table.

USING YOUR KNOWLEDGE

custom/behaviour	rules
greeting (kissing, shaking hands, etc.)	
giving gifts	
behaviour in business meetings	
business dress code	
punctuality	

3 Work in small groups. Discuss the following questions.
1 Share the information from your tables. Which rules from your tables are similar? Which are different?
2 The article discusses correct behaviour in Brazil, Japan and Saudi Arabia. What do you know about the specific customs of these countries?

WHILE READING

Annotating a text

Active readers often annotate (make notes) while reading. There are many ways to do this. You should try different techniques and choose the ones which work best for you. Below are some suggestions:

- Highlight the main ideas in a bright colour or put brackets around them.
- Highlight key words and phrases in a different colour. Use the same colours in all your annotations.
- Underline, circle or box important details such as examples, reasons and supporting arguments. In the margin, identify the type of detail you marked.

Also, as you read, write notes in the margins: summarize main ideas in your own words, outline or list important supporting details, write any questions you have, write your opinion or your reaction to the text. Working with the text in this way will help you learn and remember the important information.

4 Read the article on customs around the world on page 86 and annotate the text while you read. Part of the text has been annotated as an example.

5 Read the article again and circle the customs which are not mentioned.

a greetings
b personal space
c giving gifts
d business meetings
e table manners
f giving business cards
g being punctual

READING FOR MAIN IDEAS

CUSTOMS AROUND THE WORLD
BY ANDY SCHMIDT

1 In recent decades, foreign travel has become a multi-billion dollar industry. International travel has many benefits, but visitors can run into trouble if they don't know some basic 'rules' about the **cultures** they're visiting. It is very important for travellers to take the time to learn about the cultures they plan to visit so that they know what to **expect** and how to avoid cultural misunderstandings. That is why we are presenting this 'Customs around the world' series, where we will look at three different cultures every month to help you become a well-informed traveller. This month's exciting destinations are Brazil, Japan and Saudi Arabia.

Why learn about cultures before travel —
- *know what to expect*
- *avoid misunderstandings*

BRAZIL

2 In general, Brazilian culture is informal. Most Brazilians are very friendly people, so it is important to say hello and goodbye to the people you meet. Normally women kiss men and each other on the cheek, but men usually just shake hands. Brazilians typically stand very close to each other and touch each other's arms, elbows and back regularly while speaking. Even if this is unusual in your culture, try not to move away if this happens. If you go to a business meeting, you are not expected to take a gift. In fact, an expensive gift can be seen as suspicious[1].

Brazil– friendly, informal; greetings important

3 On the other hand, if you are invited to someone's house, you should take a gift – for example, flowers or chocolate. However, avoid anything purple or black, as these colours are related to death.

4 If you are invited to dinner, arrive at least 30 minutes late, but always dress well, because a person's **appearance** can be very important to Brazilians.

JAPAN

5 The Japanese are quite different from the Brazilians. They tend to be quite **formal**, so don't stand too close. Kissing or touching in public is not common. When you meet Japanese people socially, they may shake your hand. However, bowing, bending forwards to show respect, is the traditional greeting.

6 In a business meeting, the Japanese often like to know what your position is in your company before they talk to you. You should hand over a business card using both hands, and when you receive a business card, you should immediately read it carefully. It is important to be punctual[2]. You should arrive early and dress formally. Gifts are often **exchanged**, but the recipient may refuse the gift at least once before accepting it. You should remember to do the same if you receive a gift. When you present your gift, you should say that it is a token of your appreciation[3].

SAUDI ARABIA

7 Saudi Arabia is a very traditional country. In business situations you should know that hierarchy[4] is important to Saudis. Therefore, it is important to **greet** the oldest or the most senior person first. Men may shake hands with men, and women with women, always using the right hand. Men and women do not touch or shake hands in public.

8 Personal **relationships** are very important in Saudi Arabia. In a business meeting, do not start with business matters immediately. Instead, start by asking about people's family or health. Arrive on time for business meetings, but do not be surprised if others are late. Punctuality is less important in Saudi Arabia than it is in Japan or the US. Business dress is formal. Men should wear dark suits and ties and women should wear modest clothes.

9 Gifts are not expected at business meetings until those involved have formed a strong relationship. If you are invited to a Saudi home or office, acceptable gifts are good-quality chocolate, coffee or dates. Be careful not to admire the things the host owns, because he or she will feel obliged to give an item to you as a gift.

---

[1]**suspicious** (adj) causing a feeling of distrust or that something is wrong
[2]**punctual** (adj) on time
[3]**token of your appreciation** (n) an inexpensive gift meant to express thanks or gratitude
[4]**hierarchy** (n) status; a system for organizing people according to their importance

6 Complete the student's notes with words and phrases from the article.

READING FOR DETAIL

custom/behaviour	Brazil	Japan	Saudi Arabia
greeting	Women (1)_____ other women & men. Men (2)_____ other men.	OK to (3)_____, but (4)_____ is more traditional.	Greet (5)_____ person first. Women shake hands with (6)_____, men with (7)_____.
gifts	Bring a gift to someone's (8)_____.	Receiving: Common to (9)_____ before you accept. Giving: Say it is just a (10)_____.	Not (11)_____ at business meetings. Can bring (12)_____.
business behaviour	Do not bring a (13)_____.	Hand over your business card with (14)_____. When you receive a business card, (15)_____.	Do not (16)_____ with business matters immediately. Ask about people's (17)_____ or (18)_____.
dress/appearance	Dress (19)_____.	Dress (20)_____.	Business dress is (21)_____.
punctuality	Arrive (22)_____.	Arrive (23)_____.	Arrive (24)_____.

READING BETWEEN THE LINES

7 Work with a partner. Answer the questions.

MAKING INFERENCES

1 In Brazil, why would people probably be suspicious of an expensive gift?
   _____

2 Why shouldn't you move away if Brazilians touch you during conversation?
   _____

3 Why would Japanese business people want to know your position in a company?
   _____

4 What could be the reason why it is important to greet the oldest person first in Saudi Arabia?
   _____

5 What can be the negative result of a cultural misunderstanding?
   _____

DISCUSSION

8 Work with a partner. Discuss the questions.

1 Which of the customs in the article surprised you the most?
2 Which of the three countries has customs that are the most similar to the customs of your country? If you live in one of the countries described in the article, which customs from another country do you find most interesting? Why?

READING 2

PREPARING TO READ

UNDERSTANDING KEY VOCABULARY

1 You are going to read an article about traditional customs. Before you read the article, read the definitions below. Complete the sentences with the correct form of the words in bold.

> **belief** (n) an idea that you are sure is true
> **ceremony** (n) a formal event with special traditions, activities or words, such as a wedding
> **endangered** (adj) (of customs and traditions) in danger of being lost
> **generation** (n) all the people in a society or family who are approximately the same age
> **preserve** (v) to keep something the same or prevent it from being damaged or destroyed
> **protection** (n) the act of keeping someone or something safe from injury, damage or loss
> **tradition** (n) a belief or way of acting that people in a particular society or group have continued to follow for a long time

1 In Mexican culture, a *quinceañera* is a special _____ to celebrate a girl's 15th birthday.
2 In some cultures, several _____ live together in the same house – parents, grandparents and children.
3 Children tend to have the same _____ as their parents when they are young, but this may change when they become adults.
4 Although most Japanese cities are very modern, they still try to _____ some of their old buildings.
5 In Chinese culture, there is a _____ to give money in red envelopes at New Year.
6 Modern technology has brought many benefits, but it has also meant that some traditional customs have become _____ .
7 Places which are listed as UNESCO World Heritage sites have special _____ and cannot be destroyed.

> **Previewing a text**
>
> Before reading a text, it is a good idea to look at the title and any subtitles or photos to get a general idea of what the text is about and predict what you are going to read. This can help you to understand the text and read more quickly, especially if it contains difficult vocabulary or complicated ideas.

2 Work with a partner. Preview the article on page 90 and answer the questions.

PREVIEWING

1 Based on the title, what do you think the article will be about? Give reasons.
2 What is happening in the photos? Where were they taken?

WHILE READING

3 Read the article and annotate it. Look at page 85 for what to write.

ANNOTATING

4 Read the article and your annotations again. Then, number the points (a–e) in the order they appear (1–5).

READING FOR MAIN IDEAS

a the difference between world heritage sites and intangible cultural heritage _____
b a discussion about which customs and traditions to include in the ICH list _____
c a culture which is endangered due to the spread of cities _____
d the meaning of intangible culture _____
e a culture which has suffered due to a lack of young people _____

5 Circle the best summary of the article.
  a The article discusses efforts to preserve the world's intangible cultural heritage.
  b The article is a criticism of UNESCO's Intangible Cultural Heritage list.
  c The article is about the differences between tangible and intangible culture.

6 Identify and correct the factual mistakes in the sentences.

READING FOR DETAIL

1 UNESCO created the Intangible Cultural Heritage list in 2003.
   _____
2 The Great Barrier Reef is an example of intangible cultural heritage.
   _____
3 The women divers of Jeju Island dive for food all year round.
   _____
4 Many younger women are keeping the Jeju Haenyeo traditions alive.
   _____
5 Falconry is only practised in the United Arab Emirates.
   _____

Protecting our intangible[1] cultural heritage[2]

by Linda Barker

1. In today's ever-changing global landscape, most of us recognize the importance of preserving our own unique cultural heritage. But what do we save? A magnificent building which is under threat? A historical part of a city? An important work of art? All of these are significant, but what about our songs, stories, **ceremonies** and traditional practices? These intangible aspects of our culture can be just as meaningful as anything we build or create. Shouldn't they also be **preserved** for future generations to experience and enjoy?

2. The answer, according to UNESCO (United Nations Educational, Scientific and Cultural Organization), is yes. That is why in 2008 it published its first Intangible Cultural Heritage (ICH) list. You may already know of UNESCO's famous list of World Heritage Sites, consisting of places selected for special **protection** because of their value to the world, such as the Pyramids of Giza in Egypt or the Great Barrier Reef in Australia. However, the ICH list is different. Its purpose is to record *living* customs and **traditions** which are **endangered** by globalization. These include languages and spoken traditions (such as storytelling and poetry), performing arts, traditional crafts and local knowledge and **beliefs**.

3. Today, there are more than 400 customs and traditions on the ICH list. Two recent entries show us just how rich and varied are the practices selected for protection. The culture of the Jeju Haenyeo, the women divers of Jeju Island in South Korea, was added to the list in 2016. These amazing women dive 10 m under the sea to get food – without the use of breathing equipment. They do this for up to seven hours a day, 90 days of the year, holding their breath for about one minute every dive. Knowledge about diving practices is passed down from **generation** to generation within families. Yet today, most of the divers are in their 60s, 70s or 80s. As they have become older, younger women have not stepped in to take their place, meaning the practice is in danger of disappearing.

4. Another cultural practice added to the ICH list in the same year is falconry. This is the ancient custom of hunting with trained birds of prey, such as falcons and hawks. Regarded as both an art form and a sport, it requires years of training and discipline. Falconry is practised around the world from France to Mongolia to the United Arab Emirates, which is home to the world's first falcon hospital and each year hosts a falcon 'beauty contest'. Sadly, falconry is now threatened by the growth of cities and the loss of natural habitats. There are fears that the practice may disappear unless efforts to preserve it are successful.

5. Both Jeju Haenyeo and falconry illustrate the tremendous range of cultural practices which the ICH list was created to preserve. And yet, while most of us would agree that UNESCO's efforts are valuable, I find myself questioning the fairness and usefulness of the ICH list. Why are some customs and practices included while others are not? Who decides this? Does inclusion on the list make a difference in the long term? In this age of rapid globalization, when fewer young people are interested in learning about the customs of their ancestors, it may already be too late to preserve much of our diverse and precious cultural heritage. But for the benefit of future generations, I believe we must never stop trying.

[1] **intangible** (adj) something which exists although you cannot touch it
[2] **heritage** (n) traditions, languages or buildings belonging to the culture of a particular society which were created in the past and still have importance

READING BETWEEN THE LINES

7 Work with a partner. Answer the questions.

MAKING INFERENCES

1 What is the difference between tangible and intangible culture?
   _____

2 What are the reasons why so many intangible traditions are dying out?
   _____

3 Why did UNESCO create the Intangible Cultural Heritage list?
   _____

4 Does the author believe UNESCO's work is important? How do you know?
   _____

DISCUSSION

8 Work with a partner. Use ideas from Reading 1 and Reading 2 to answer the following questions.

SYNTHESIZING

1 Can local customs and practices compete with globalization?
2 In a globalized world, which customs are most likely to survive and which will probably disappear?
3 What can countries do to preserve their living cultural heritage? What is your country doing?

🔵 LANGUAGE DEVELOPMENT

AVOIDING GENERALIZATIONS

GRAMMAR

In academic English, be careful not to make generalizations unless you have details to support them. For instance, a reader of the example sentence below could argue that not all cultural traditions change.
All cultural traditions change.
You can avoid generalizations by using words such as *many*, *can* or *tend to*.

Quantifier
Many cultural traditions change.

Verb
Cultural traditions tend to change.

Modal verb
Cultural traditions can change.

1 Read the generalizations about common customs. Then, use the words in brackets to make the sentences more accurate.

1 We tip the waiter in restaurants. (tend to)
   _____

2 Brazilian culture is informal. (tend to)
   _____

3 Expensive gifts look suspicious. (can)
   _____

4 Common hand gestures like waving are misunderstood in a different culture. (can)
   _____

5 In the Middle East, old people live with their children. (many)
   _____

ADVERBS OF FREQUENCY TO AVOID GENERALIZATIONS

> **GRAMMAR**
>
> You can also use adverbs of frequency to avoid generalizations.
>
> 0% → 100%
>
> | never | seldom / hardly ever / rarely | occasionally / sometimes | often | usually / almost always / normally / frequently | always |
>
> Adverbs go before the main verb, but after the verb *to be* in a sentence.
>
> *In Tokyo, people **usually** go to work by train or bus.*
> *Formal dinner parties **are often** difficult to organize.*

2 Read the generalizations and use the adverbs in brackets to make the sentences more accurate.

1 Brazilian men shake hands, though it is not unusual for men to kiss each other on the cheek. (usually)
   _____

2 Saudi men wear traditional clothing, even to business meetings. (often)
   _____

3 Professionals get upset if you don't use their correct title. (sometimes)
   _____

4 Cultural knowledge is helpful in business situations. (frequently)
   _____

5 In Japan, you should arrive on time for an appointment. (always)
   _____

SYNONYMS TO AVOID REPETITION

3 Replace the words in bold in the sentences with the synonyms in the box.

| brief   certain   common   important   obvious   separate   serious |

1 The business meeting was **short**, and we went straight to the reception for our overseas visitors. _____
2 The high cost of education is a **bad** problem for many families. _____
3 In many cultures, parents and their married children live in **different** houses. _____
4 In **some** countries, cooking traditional food is becoming less popular. _____
5 There were several **powerful** people at the event. _____
6 Some customs and traditions are not **clear** to people who are visiting a country for the first time. _____
7 It is **usual** for people in my country to have large families. _____

WRITING

CRITICAL THINKING

At the end of this unit, you will write a summary paragraph and a response paragraph about Reading 2. Look at this unit's writing task below.

> Write a summary paragraph about Reading 2 in this unit. Then, write a response paragraph giving your opinion about the efforts to preserve the world's intangible cultural heritage.

ANALYZE

1 Look again at Reading 2 on page 90. Then, answer the questions by writing notes in the table below.

1 What was the main idea of Reading 2? Write your answer in the space for paragraph 1.
2 Look at each paragraph of Reading 2. Write some notes about the main idea and supporting details for each paragraph.
3 What was the author's conclusion? Write it in your own words.
(Tip: The main idea and conclusion are often similar.)

paragraph	main idea	details	my response
1 introduction			
2	ICH list was established to protect living customs and practices.	List includes languages, spoken traditions, performing arts, crafts, knowledge and beliefs.	
3			
4			
5 conclusion			

Responding to an author's ideas

One way of responding to a text you have read is to address the author's main ideas with your own point of view. How you respond will depend on how you feel about each point. Some common ways people respond to an author's ideas are:

- Agreeing or disagreeing with the author's points or ideas
- Giving an example from your own experience or of someone you know
- Connecting the author's ideas to something you read or heard from another source
- Providing a different opinion about the same issue
- Evaluating the point or idea. For example, saying whether you think that it is positive or negative

2 Write your responses to each part of Reading 2 in the table on the opposite page. Use the points in the skill box as a guide.

EVALUATE

GRAMMAR FOR WRITING

PARAPHRASING

Paraphrasing means rewriting someone else's ideas in your own words. This skill is important, especially when writing essays, because copying another person's exact words without referring to the source is *plagiarism* (stealing someone's ideas).

To paraphrase, begin by reading the original text. For example:

International travel has many benefits, but visitors can run into trouble if they don't know some basic 'rules' about the cultures they are visiting (Schmidt, 2018).

Then, use one or more of the following strategies to paraphrase the original. Remember to include the source of your information, even when you are paraphrasing.

Replace words or phrases with synonyms.	Foreign travel has many advantages, but travellers can have problems unless they spend time learning the customs of the places they are visiting (Schmidt, 2018).
Change the order of some words or phrases.	Foreign travel has many advantages, but unless travellers learn about the customs of the places they are visiting, they can have problems (Schmidt, 2018).
Use indirect speech. *According to X, …*	**According to** Schmidt (2018), foreign travel has many advantages, but …
X *states / writes / believes / says (that)* …*	Schmidt (2018) **states that** foreign travel has many advantages, but …

*The word *that* is often left out after *believes* and *says*

1 Read the second paragraph on page 86 and the paraphrases (1–3) below. Match the paraphrase with the strategy (a–c) the writer used.

Original text: Brazilians typically stand very close to each other and touch each other's arms, elbows and back regularly while speaking. (Schmidt, 2018)

1 According to Schmidt (2018), Brazilians tend to stand very close to each other and touch each other's arms, elbows and back regularly while speaking.
2 Brazilian people tend to stand quite close to one another, and they frequently touch each other on the upper body while they are talking (Schmidt, 2018).
3 While they are talking, Brazilian people tend to stand very close to one another and touch each other's backs, arms or elbows frequently (Schmidt, 2018).

a use synonyms
b change the order of words or phrases
c use indirect speech

2 Paraphrase the sentences from Reading 2 using the strategy in brackets.

1 In today's ever-changing global landscape, most of us recognize the importance of preserving our own unique cultural heritage. (use synonyms)
_____
_____
_____

2 Sadly, falconry is now threatened by the growth of cities and the loss of natural habitats. (use synonyms and change the order of words or phrases)
_____
_____
_____

3 In this age of rapid globalization, when fewer young people are interested in learning about the customs of their ancestors, it may already be too late to preserve much of our diverse and precious cultural heritage (Barker, 2018). (use all three techniques)
_____
_____
_____

3 Work with a partner. Compare your paraphrases. Can you make any improvements?

ACADEMIC WRITING SKILLS

WRITING A SUMMARY AND A PERSONAL RESPONSE

Writing a summary and a personal response is an opportunity to evaluate and express opinions about a writer's ideas.

A **summary** is a short paragraph which paraphrases the main ideas and important points of a longer text. You should always write a summary in your own words, but be sure not to change the original author's ideas. The paragraph should not include your opinion.

In a **response** paragraph you should give your ideas about the points in the summary. Your response can include examples from your personal experience, facts or knowledge from other sources. You can use the following expressions:

I agree/disagree with the author that … because …
In my opinion, …
I think that …
In my experience, …

1 Read Reading 1 on page 86 again. Then, read a student's summary and response below. Answer the questions which follow on page 98.

Summary and response

In the article 'Customs around the world', Schmidt (2018) says it is important for travellers to learn about the customs of other countries in order to prevent cultural misunderstandings in the places they are visiting. Schmidt focuses on three countries – Brazil, Japan and Saudi Arabia – and describes some customs visitors should know about. According to the author, Brazilians are informal people. They touch a lot, and punctuality is not expected on most occasions. Japanese culture is exactly the opposite. People don't touch in public, and there are rules for how to exchange business cards, how to dress, what kind of gifts to give and when to arrive at a meeting or someone's home. Saudi culture is also formal. For example, women and men are not allowed to touch each other in public. The author stresses the importance of personal relationships and warns us that it is important to spend time asking about a host's family or health, before starting to talk about business matters.

I definitely agree with Schmidt's main point: it is easy to make a mistake if you don't know about other people's customs. To give an example from my own experience, I was travelling in India when I was invited to dinner at a friend's home. I had never been to an Indian home, so I decided to do some reading about a proper gift to bring. One of the things I learnt is that a guest should not bring white flowers, because white is associated with death. Reading this information before the event prevented me from making an embarrassing mistake. In short, these examples remind us that travellers must study the customs of a new country before visiting it.

1 Which sentence restates the main idea in Reading 1 on page 86?
___

2 Compare the main idea sentence in Reading 1 and the main idea sentence of the summary paragraph. Which paraphrasing strategies from the box on page 95 did the summary writer use?
___

3 What other information from Reading 1 did the writer include in the summary paragraph?
___

4 Which examples from Reading 1 did the writer include in the summary? Do you think this is too much, too little or the right amount of detail?
___

5 How many references to the author are there in the summary paragraph? Underline them.

6 Where does the writer give her opinion? Underline the sentence.

7 How does the writer support her opinion?
___

8 How does the writer conclude the essay? What transition does she use?
___

2 Compare answers with a partner and make any necessary changes.

WRITING TASK

▌Write a summary paragraph about Reading 2 in this unit. Then, write a response paragraph giving your opinion about the efforts to preserve the world's intangible cultural heritage.

PLAN

1 Look at the table you created in Exercises 1 and 2 in the Critical thinking section. Then, complete an outline for your summary and response paragraphs, using the following structure.

Summary paragraph
topic sentence (author's main idea): _____
_____

supporting detail 1:
_____
_____

supporting detail 2:
_____
_____

supporting detail 3:
_____
_____

Response paragraph
topic sentence (your reaction to the author's main idea): _____
_____

supporting detail 1:
_____
_____

supporting detail 2:
_____
_____

supporting detail 3 (optional):
_____
_____

concluding sentence (restates your opinion):
_____
_____

2 Review the Task checklist on page 100 as you prepare your paragraphs.

WRITE A FIRST DRAFT

3 Write your summary paragraph and personal response paragraph.

REVISE

4 Use the Task checklist to review your paragraphs for content and structure.

TASK CHECKLIST	✔
Did you restate the author's main idea in your own words?	
Did you summarize the important details which support the main idea?	
Did you give examples or other supporting details for your opinion in the response paragraph?	
Did you restate your opinion in the concluding sentence?	

5 Make any necessary changes to your paragraphs.

EDIT

6 Use the Language checklist to edit your paragraphs for language errors.

LANGUAGE CHECKLIST	✔
Did you use quantifiers, verbs and modals to avoid generalizations?	
Did you use adverbs of frequency correctly?	
Did you replace adjectives with synonyms to avoid repetition?	
Did you use paraphrasing to rewrite someone else's ideas?	

7 Make any necessary changes to your paragraphs.

OBJECTIVES REVIEW

1 Check your learning objectives for this unit. Write *3*, *2* or *1* for each objective.

   3 = very well   2 = well   1 = not so well

   I can ...

   watch and understand a video about the Coming of Age Day in South Korea. _____

   annotate a text. _____

   preview a text. _____

   respond to an author's ideas. _____

   avoid generalizations. _____

   use adverbs of frequency to avoid generalizations. _____

   paraphrase. _____

   write a summary and a personal response. _____

   write a summary paragraph and a response paragraph. _____

2 Use the *Unlock* Digital Workbook for more practice with this unit's learning objectives.

WORDLIST

appearance (n) ◉	endangered (adj)	obvious (adj) ◉
belief (n) ◉	exchange (v) ◉	preserve (v) ◉
brief (adj) ◉	expect (v) ◉	protection (n) ◉
ceremony (n)	formal (adj) ◉	relationship (n) ◉
certain (adj) ◉	generation (n) ◉	separate (adj) ◉
common (adj) ◉	greet (v)	serious (adj) ◉
culture (n) ◉	important (adj) ◉	tradition (n) ◉

◉ = high-frequency words in the Cambridge Academic Corpus

LEARNING OBJECTIVES	IN THIS UNIT YOU WILL ...
Watch and listen	watch and understand a video about the amount of sugar in food and drinks.
Reading skill	make inferences.
Critical thinking	support an argument.
Grammar	use verb and noun forms; state opinions; state a purpose; link contrasting sentences.
Academic writing skill	structure an essay (introductory, body and concluding paragraphs).
Writing task	write a balanced opinion essay.

HEALTH AND FITNESS

UNIT 5

UNLOCK YOUR KNOWLEDGE

Work with a partner. Discuss the questions.

1 Look at the photo. Do you think this is a good way to stay fit and healthy? Why / Why not?
2 What are some habits of healthy people?
3 What things do healthy people usually avoid?
4 What kinds of things can people do to keep fit?

WATCH AND LISTEN

PREPARING TO WATCH

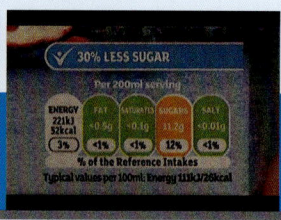

ACTIVATING YOUR KNOWLEDGE

1 Work with a partner. Discuss the questions.

1 Do you eat any foods which contain a lot of sugar? If so, which ones?
2 Which kinds of food and drink contain a lot of added sugar?
3 Do you read the information on food labels? Why / Why not?

PREDICTING CONTENT USING VISUALS

2 Work with a partner. You are going to watch a news report. Before you watch, look at the photos. What do you think the report will be about?

GLOSSARY

consumption/intake (n) the amount of something that someone uses, eats or drinks

manufacturer (n) a company that produces goods in large numbers

under pressure (phr) Someone is under pressure when somebody else tries to make them do something they do not want to do.

reluctant (adj) not wanting to do something and therefore slow to do it

campaigner (n) somebody who does activities to try to change something, such as a law, in society

WHILE WATCHING

UNDERSTANDING MAIN IDEAS

3 ▶ Watch the video. Which statement best describes the main idea of the video?

1 People are getting too fat because they eat a lot of sugary foods without knowing it.
2 Food manufacturers add a lot of sugar to food and campaigners want to change that.
3 A new law has been made that manufacturers must tell customers how much sugar is in their food.

4 ▶ Watch again. Complete the missing numbers according to the information in the video.

> UK adults eat ¹_____ pounds (= 3 kg) of sugar a month.
> - *Alpen Trail Bar* has ²_____ teaspoons of sugar, ³_____ added.
> - *Nestlé Munch Bunch* drink has ⁴_____ teaspoons of sugar, ⁵_____ added.
> - *Quaker Oat So Simple* porridge with fruit has ⁶_____ teaspoons of sugar.
>
> Campaigners think adults should get ⁷_____ of their energy from sugar.

UNDERSTANDING DETAIL

5 Write the correct form of the words in bold next to the definitions below.

Some of it comes **naturally** from the ingredients in our food …

The labels don't **differentiate** so we've done some of our own research.

The company won't **disclose** how much of that is added.

When you remove any food **component** that **delivers** flavour, um, you've got to do it slowly and **gradually**, so you train the customer's **palate** to accept that change.

_____ add; bring
_____ ingredient
_____ not made or done by people
_____ slowly over a period of time
_____ to show the difference between things
_____ the ability you use to decide if you like a taste
_____ to give information that was secret

WORKING OUT MEANING FROM CONTEXT

6 ▶ Watch again. Work with a partner. Discuss the questions.
 1 Why did the news team decide to do some research?
 2 Why might a food or drink manufacturer not want to talk about added sugar?
 3 Why do you think the scientific report's recommendations are important?

MAKING INFERENCES

DISCUSSION

7 Work in small groups. Discuss the questions.
 1 What information do you think food manufacturers should have to put on their labels? Why?
 2 Do you think that scientific advice makes a difference to what people choose to eat and drink? Give some examples.

READING

READING 1

PREPARING TO READ

UNDERSTANDING KEY VOCABULARY

1 Before you read the article, read the sentences (1–7) below and write the words in bold next to the definitions (a–g).

1 Heart disease is an extremely **serious** condition. Many people die each year from this illness.
2 Playing team sports is an excellent way to raise the **self-esteem** of teenagers. It helps them to feel confident and happy with themselves.
3 My grandmother is 88 years old, but she is still quite **active**. She walks every day and even plays tennis twice a week.
4 To lose weight, you should get more exercise and eat fewer **calories**.
5 To stay healthy, you should do a **moderate** amount of exercise each week. Two and a half hours a week is the right amount.
6 Many young people do not **recognize** the importance of getting enough sleep.
7 I have decided to **reduce** the amount of sugar I eat. Now I have dessert only once a week.

a _____ (adj) doing things which involve moving and using energy
b _____ (v) to limit; to use less of something
c _____ (adj) bad or dangerous
d _____ (n) being confident and believing in yourself
e _____ (n pl) the measurement of the amount of energy found in food
f _____ (v) to understand; to accept that something is true
g _____ (adj) not too much and not too little

PREDICTING CONTENT USING VISUALS

2 Write the names of the types of activity shown in the photos.

a _____   b _____   c _____   d _____

e _____   f _____   g _____   h _____

1. How much physical activity do you do in a week? Are you getting enough exercise? Regular activity benefits your health in many ways. For example, people who exercise regularly are less likely to suffer from many chronic diseases[1], such as heart disease, type 2 diabetes[2], stroke[3] and some cancers. Experts say adults who exercise for just 150 minutes a week can **reduce** their risk of **serious** illness by 50%. In addition, regular exercise increases life expectancy[4] and reduces the risk of early death by 30%. It also improves your mood, **self-esteem** and sleep quality.

2. Today, most adults are much less **active** than in the past because our jobs are far less physical than the work our grandparents used to do. In fact, many of us spend seven hours or more just sitting in a chair each day. This lack of regular physical activity means that people burn fewer **calories** than in the past, so we need to make an extra effort to use up all our energy. According to experts, adults need to do two and a half hours of **moderate** exercise per week. This could be fast walking or cycling on a flat road. In addition, it is important to do exercises to strengthen muscles two or three times a week.

3. Exercise can be expensive, but it doesn't have to be. Team sports, such as football or basketball, can be cheap because all the players share the cost of the field or court. Joining a recreational sports league is usually an inexpensive way of getting exercise and can be very social, too. Local leisure centres usually offer squash and badminton at low rates if you book a court at off-peak times, and you may be able to get a reduced-price gym membership, too.

4. If you don't want to spend any money at all, try one of the following activities. Go for a run; the only equipment you need is a pair of running shoes. If you take the bus, try getting off one stop early and walking the extra distance. Go to the park. Try getting a group of friends or family together for a game of football, or play the kinds of running games you haven't played since you were a child. This is a great way to involve the whole family and also help you keep fit. Alternatively, if you want to stay at home, gardening or doing housework are great ways to keep fit, and you can enjoy the benefit of a nice garden and a tidy house, too!

5. Although adults should do two and a half hours of exercise a week, you don't have to do it all at one time. Split the time into ten-minute chunks! If you do ten minutes before work, ten minutes during your lunch break and ten minutes after work, five days a week, you've achieved the target! You could also go swimming during your lunch hour two or three times a week and you've done it! In brief, there are many easy ways of keeping fit. If we all **recognize** the value of doing this, we will live longer and be healthier.

---

[1]**chronic disease** (n) a disease that lasts a long time
[2]**diabetes** (n) a disease in which the body is not able to use sugar efficiently
[3]**stroke** (n) a medical condition in which blood cannot reach the brain and the brain becomes damaged
[4]**life expectancy** (n) the number of years that a person can expect to live

SKIMMING

READING FOR MAIN IDEAS

READING FOR DETAIL

WHILE READING

3 Skim the magazine article and circle the best title.

  a Get some exercise and lose weight at the same time!
  b Walking to improve your health and mood.
  c Keep fit! It's easier than you might think.

4 Read the article. Match the headings (a–e) below to the paragraphs (1–5) in the article.

  a But I can't afford gym membership! _____
  b Exercise regularly to stay healthy. _____
  c But I don't have time! _____
  d Get out of your chair! _____
  e Exercise can be free. _____

5 Read the article again and answer the questions.

  1 Which four medical problems can be avoided with regular exercise?
     _____ , _____ , _____ , _____
  2 Which other three things does exercise improve?
     _____ , _____ , _____
  3 How much time do some adults spend each day sitting down?
     _____
  4 What do team sport players share the cost of? _____
  5 When should you book a racquetball court for cheap rates?
     _____
  6 What equipment do you need for running? _____
  7 Where should you go to exercise and spend time with your family?
     _____

READING BETWEEN THE LINES

Making inferences

Making inferences is a very important academic skill. It means using your knowledge and clues in the text to guess about things which aren't stated in the text but are probably true. For example:

Research shows that running burns more calories per minute than swimming.

Question: What sport would be better for busy people?   **Answer:** Running

People who are busy have less time, but still want to get fit. Running helps them to become fitter more quickly.

When reading academic texts, you may be asked to make inferences about the writer's purpose, background or attitude. Making inferences is part of being a good reader. It allows you to gain a deeper understanding of the text.

6 Read the article again and answer the questions.

1 How do you think exercise improves self-esteem?
   _____

2 Is the article written for adults or for children? How do you know?
   _____

MAKING INFERENCES

DISCUSSION

7 Work with a partner. Discuss the questions.

1 Look at the photos on page 106. Do you do any of these activities?
2 Is sport the best way to keep fit? Why / Why not?
3 Is exercise ever a bad thing? Why / Why not?

READING 2

PREPARING TO READ

1 Read the definitions and complete the sentences with the correct form of the words in bold.

UNDERSTANDING KEY VOCABULARY

> **balanced diet** (n) a daily eating programme which has a healthy mixture of different kinds of food
> **campaign** (n) a group of activities designed to motivate people to take action, such as giving money or changing their behaviour
> **junk food** (n) food which is unhealthy but quick and easy to eat
> **nutritional** (adj) relating to food and the way it affects your health
> **obesity** (n) the condition of weighing more than is healthy
> **portion** (n) the amount of food served to one person

1 I try to eat a _____ consisting of a little meat, some dairy products and a lot of fruit, vegetables and grains.
2 I love _____ like crisps and hot dogs, but I'm careful not to eat too much of those foods because I know they aren't good for me.
3 _____ is a serious problem all over the world. In some countries, more than 50% of adults are overweight.
4 One way to lose weight is to eat the same foods but smaller _____ .
5 Right now, my company is sponsoring a _____ to raise money for a new gym in the local school.
6 Snacks like sweets and crisps have little _____ value. Having fruit or raw vegetables is much better for your body.

USING YOUR KNOWLEDGE

2 Work with a partner. Answer the questions.
  1 What percentage of a healthy diet do you think should be:
    a fruit and vegetables? _____
    b carbohydrates? _____
    c dairy products? _____
    d proteins? _____
  2 What are some ways governments can help people avoid obesity?
  3 What can individuals do to stay healthy and prevent obesity?

SCANNING TO PREDICT CONTENT

3 Scan the essay on page 111 and check your answers to the questions in Exercise 2.

WHILE READING

READING FOR MAIN IDEAS

4 Read the essay. Then, read the list of measures (a–h) the writer describes for preventing or reducing obesity. Write G (government) or I (individuals) to show who the writer believes should take responsibility.
  a ____ organize educational campaigns to encourage people to eat a low-calorie, balanced diet
  b ____ control portion size
  c ____ eat a balanced diet
  d ____ read nutritional information on food packaging
  e ____ list calorie counts on menu items in restaurants
  f ____ eat only small amounts of sweet foods
  g ____ put a tax on foods which are high in fat and sugar
  h ____ do exercise

READING FOR DETAIL

5 Look at the supporting details in the table below and write the measures from Exercise 4 next to the details which support them.

measures	supporting detail
1	Information can help people make intelligent food choices. ____
2	Healthy diet = 50% fruit and veg; 30% carbs; 15% protein; 5% dairy ____
3	Makes junk food too expensive to buy in large quantities. ____
4 control portion size	Average man needs around 2,500 calories per day. Average woman requires around 2,000. __F__
5	Exercise burns calories. ____

6 Work with a partner. Which kinds of details does the author use to support the arguments in paragraphs 2 and 3? Write F (fact), E (example) or R (reason) next to the supporting details in the table above.

Whose responsibility is it to fight obesity: individuals or the government? Discuss both sides of the argument and give your opinion.

1 **Obesity** has become a major problem in many parts of the world. According to the World Health Organization (WHO), in 2016 about 13% of adults, both male and female, were obese. Moreover, the percentage of obese people increased by 300% between 1975 and 2016. Obesity can cause major health problems like heart disease, diabetes, stroke and breathing problems. Tackling[1] obesity is a big task. Whose responsibility should it be? Although some people say it is up to individuals to manage their own weight, others believe governments should take the lead by making laws designed to help reduce the obesity problem.

2 On the one hand, many people insist that individuals are the ones who need to take the major responsibility for controlling their own weight. Supporters of this position have explained how we can do this. First, we can control the size of the **portions** we eat. An average man needs around 2,500 calories per day, while an average woman requires around 2,000. Moreover, we should learn how to eat a **balanced diet** consisting of a variety of foods in order to maintain a healthy weight. In many Western countries, for example, a typical healthy diet might include approximately 50% fruit and vegetables; 30% carbohydrates, such as bread, rice, potatoes and pasta; 15% proteins, for example, meat, fish, eggs and beans; and around 5% dairy products (e.g. milk and cheese). Next, we all need to read the **nutritional** information on food packaging. This would help us to control our intake of unhealthy ingredients like sugar and saturated fats[2] and make intelligent food choices. And finally, each of us should make time to exercise because, as we all know, exercise burns calories.

3 On the other hand, some people insist that individual efforts to control obesity often end in failure. They argue that governments should take the lead in fighting obesity. They propose a number of measures. First, many countries already have laws requiring nutritional information on packaged foods. Supporters of this law think large restaurant chains should also list calorie counts, as well as the amount of cholesterol[3], on their menus. This information can help customers choose low-calorie, nutritious food even when they are not cooking at home. Next, many people support a tax on foods which are high in fat and sugar, such as pizza, crisps, chocolate and sweets. Such a tax would make **junk food** too expensive for people to buy in large quantities. Finally, many people strongly believe that governments should support educational **campaigns** to encourage people to eat a low-calorie, balanced diet. Such campaigns would be similar to the anti-smoking campaigns that have helped reduce the number of smokers all over the world.

4 In conclusion, there are strong arguments for governments and individuals taking increased responsibility for tackling the obesity crisis. In my opinion, both parties have a role to play in dealing with this global problem. Governments should pass new laws and provide education to encourage people to choose healthier lifestyles. At the same time, individuals have to take more responsibility for their meal choices and choose healthier foods and smaller portions. If we really wish to see an end to the problem of obesity in the future, individuals and governments must both take action.

[1]**tackle** (v) to deal with something
[2]**saturated fat** (n) an unhealthy fat which contains higher proportions of fatty acid
[3]**cholesterol** (n) a fatty substance found in all animal cells – high levels can block arteries and cause heart disease

7 Read the essay again to look for the examples of these food types in the table.

food type	examples
carbohydrates	1 bread,
dairy products	2
proteins	3
high-fat foods	4
sugary foods	5

READING BETWEEN THE LINES

MAKING INFERENCES

8 Would the writer agree or disagree with these claims? Write *A* (agree) or *D* (disagree). Then, underline the sections of the essay which support your answers.

1 Obesity is a serious problem only in Western countries. _____
2 A balanced meal will not have the same foods in every country. _____
3 Campaigns aimed at getting people to stop smoking have been successful in many countries. _____
4 Eating a balanced diet is enough on its own to help people manage their weight and stay healthy. _____
5 Governments have a greater responsibility than individuals to help people avoid obesity. _____

DISCUSSION

SYNTHESIZING

9 Work with a partner. Use ideas from Reading 1 and Reading 2 to answer the following questions.

1 Which is more important for good health: a regular exercise programme or a balanced diet? Why?
2 Many people work hard and get a lot of exercise in their jobs, but they are still obese. Why do you think that happens?
3 Do you think that adverts for junk food should be illegal? Why / Why not?
4 Do you agree that governments should tax products that are bad for our health, or do you think people should be free to make their own decisions?

LANGUAGE DEVELOPMENT

VERB AND NOUN FORMS

> **GRAMMAR**
>
> You will be able to read faster and with better comprehension if you can recognize the verb and noun forms of words. The two forms can be the same or different.
>
> The biggest thing that stops people going to the gym is the **cost**. (noun)
> Gym membership should **cost** less so more people can join. (verb)
> We need to find a **solution** to the problem of childhood obesity. (noun)
> We need to **solve** the problem of childhood obesity. (verb)

1 Look at the verbs in the box and underline their noun forms in the paragraph.

> advertise   ban   encourage   promote
> protect   recognize   reduce

> We need to see a reduction in the rate of obesity among children and teenagers. The first step is recognition that fat is a real problem for young people. One solution is for schools to offer children the opportunity to participate in sport. This would require the involvement and encouragement of parents, who are our main weapon against increasing obesity. Parents can also support the promotion of educational campaigns to teach children about healthy eating.
> All of us should be responsible for the protection of our own health, but governments can also help fight the obesity problem. For example, they can impose a ban on junk food adverts aimed at children.

HEALTH AND FITNESS COLLOCATIONS

VOCABULARY

Collocations are pairs of words which frequently occur together, for example, *noun + noun* or *adjective + noun*. Collocations sound correct to fluent speakers of a language. For example, *heart disease* sounds correct. On the other hand, *heart illness* sounds wrong, even though we can understand the meaning. Using the right collocations can help you speak and write English more naturally.

2 Look at the paragraph and underline ten collocations (*noun + noun* or *adjective + noun*) related to health and fitness. The first one has been done for you as an example.

> Obesity can reduce <u>life expectancy</u> and lead to serious illness such as heart disease and diabetes. To address this problem, some governments run educational programmes and advertising campaigns. These educate people about the dangers of junk food and the importance of a balanced diet. They also show people how to find out about the nutritional value of food. Another important way to tackle obesity is regular exercise, because the more physical activity we have, the better we feel.

PLUS

3 Now complete the table by writing the correct collocation next to the definition.

definition		collocation
how long a person can expect to live	1	life expectancy
how good a particular kind of food is for you	2	
classes or material to teach people about a particular topic	3	
an illness of the heart	4	
moving around and doing things	5	
media projects to convince people to buy a product or change their behaviour	6	
a very bad medical problem	7	
a healthy mixture of different types of food	8	
sport or movement that people do at the same time each day, week, month, etc.	9	
food that is unhealthy but is quick and easy to eat	10	

WRITING

CRITICAL THINKING

At the end of this unit, you will write a balanced opinion essay. Look at this unit's writing task below.

> Should universities require students to take physical education classes? Discuss both sides and give your opinion.

SKILLS

Supporting an argument

When you plan a balanced opinion essay, make a list of arguments. Then, list ideas for and against each argument. This will help you think about your own opinions and how you will support your position. A balanced opinion essay must include arguments which support each side of the issue. Be sure to support your arguments with specific details – facts, examples, reasons, personal experience, etc. Such details will make your arguments stronger.

1 Look back at paragraph 3 of Reading 2 on page 111. In your own words, complete the list of arguments the author gives and the details she uses to support this position.

UNDERSTAND

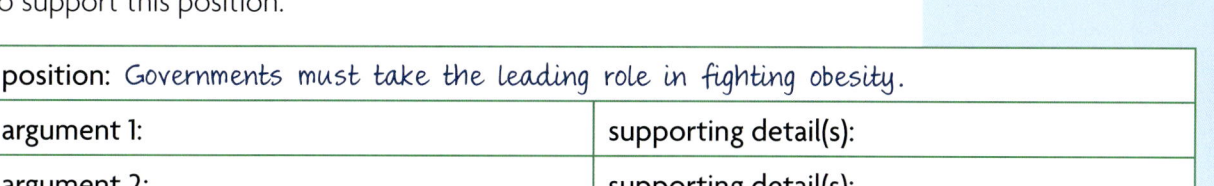

position: *Governments must take the leading role in fighting obesity.*	
argument 1:	supporting detail(s):
argument 2:	supporting detail(s):
argument 3:	supporting detail(s):

2 Work with a partner. Look at the writing task. Make a list of arguments for and against this proposal.

REMEMBER

topic: *Universities should require students to take physical education classes.*	
arguments for:	arguments against:
Exercise decreases stress.	*Students are busy, and physical education classes reduce study time.*

APPLY

3 Work with a partner. Compare your tables and add any relevant information to your own table.

4 Review your arguments in the table on page 115 and decide if you will argue for or against the topic. Write your opinion at the bottom of the table below. Then, choose two arguments for and two arguments against. Copy them and make notes on the details you will use to support them.

argument for 1:	supporting detail(s):
argument for 2:	supporting detail(s):
argument against 1:	supporting detail(s):
argument against 2:	supporting detail(s):
my opinion (with reasons):	

ANALYZE

5 Work with a partner. Compare and contrast your arguments and supporting details. Make any changes to your table as necessary.

GRAMMAR FOR WRITING

STATING OPINIONS

Successful writers clearly state their opinions when they write an opinion essay. You can state your opinion with opinion phrases or with modals. Remember to support your opinion with details.

opinion phrases In my opinion, In my view, I believe (that) I think (that)	**In my opinion,** both parties have a role to play in dealing with this global problem.
modals should / shouldn't ought to need to / don't need to must / don't have to	The government **needs to** play a larger role in fighting obesity. Individuals **ought to** make better food choices.

Notice how writers often use different words to mean *think* when they present their opinion about an argument. This helps avoid repetition.

Many people	think argue believe claim feel insist state suggest	that individuals should be responsible for their own health.

1 Read the questions and answer them with an opinion phrase. Then, give reasons for your opinion. Try to use different words for *think*.

1 Should junk food adverts be illegal?
   _____

2 Is running the best exercise for keeping fit?
   _____

3 Is it necessary to sleep eight hours a night in order to stay healthy?
   _____

2 Work with a partner. Compare your answers. Do you agree or disagree?

3 Fill in the gaps with a modal. Use the affirmative or negative form according to your opinion. Use a different expression in each sentence.

1 Governments _____ control junk food advertising on television.
2 Children _____ start learning about good nutrition in primary school.
3 Governments _____ tax foods which contain sugar.
4 Most people _____ exercise ten hours a week.
5 Food packages _____ have labels which provide nutritional information.

STATING A PURPOSE

When you support an argument by stating a purpose, you can use *to* or *in order to*. Both are followed by an infinitive.

Governments should promote healthy eating	to	increase life expectancy.
	in order to	

You can also use *so* or *so that*. These are usually followed by a clause with *can*.

Governments should build more leisure centres	so	people can play more sport.
	so that	

4 Complete the sentences using *to, in order to, so* or *so that*. In some items, more than one answer is possible.

1 Governments need to increase the tax on junk food _____ make it more expensive.
2 Nutrition labels should be added to food packaging _____ people can see if their food is healthy or not.
3 Governments should provide free sports clubs _____ people living in poorer areas can participate in sports.
4 Governments should promote the idea of eating five portions of fruit and vegetables per day _____ improve people's diets.
5 Some people argue that junk food advertising should be banned _____ children are not influenced by it.

LINKING CONTRASTING SENTENCES

> Use *but*, *however* and *on the other hand* before a new idea that is opposed to, or in contrast to, the first idea. Use *although* before the first idea.
>
> first idea
> <u>Some people say it is up to individuals to manage their own weight</u>.
> contrasting idea
> **However**, <u>others believe governments should take the lead</u>.
>
> first idea
> **Although** <u>some people say it is up to individuals to manage their own weight,</u>
> contrasting idea
> <u>others believe governments should take the lead</u>.

5 Look at the statements (1–4) and circle the linking expression in each one. Then, look at the punctuation between the two contrasting ideas. How is it different? Write *C* (comma) or *F* (full stop).

1 Some people feel that governments should be responsible for controlling the obesity problem, but others claim that people need to manage their own health. _____
2 Some people feel that governments should be responsible for controlling the obesity problem, although others claim that people need to manage their own health. _____
3 Some people feel that governments should be responsible for controlling the obesity problem. However, others claim that people need to manage their own health. _____
4 Some people feel that governments should be responsible for controlling the obesity problem. On the other hand, others claim that people need to manage their own health. _____

6 Rewrite the sentences below using *although*. The first one has been done for you as an example. More than one answer is possible.

1 Meat and fish are healthy foods, **but** they are expensive in most countries.
   <u>Although meat and fish are healthy foods, they are expensive in most countries.</u>
2 Some forms of exercise, such as running, are free. However, many people never exercise. _____
   _____
3 Junk-food advertising on TV is exciting for children. However, it can have a negative influence on their eating habits. _____
   _____
4 Most adults should exercise for at least two hours every week, but they don't have to do it all at once. _____
   _____

ACADEMIC WRITING SKILLS

ESSAY STRUCTURE

An essay is a series of connected paragraphs that discuss one main topic. Essays have three important parts:

— An **introductory paragraph** presents the topic, gives background information and shows the organization of the essay. The last sentence of the introductory paragraph gives a **thesis statement**, which explains what the body paragraphs will be about.

— **Body paragraphs** explain or develop the thesis statement. Each body paragraph starts with a topic sentence that links back to the thesis statement. Each body paragraph provides supporting details to its topic sentence. In a balanced opinion essay, the writer must explain both sides of an argument.

— A **concluding paragraph** restates the thesis statement and provides the writer's own thoughts on the topic. In a balanced opinion essay, the concluding paragraph summarizes both arguments, states the writer's opinion and may conclude with a prediction about the future or a recommendation for action.

1 Look back at Reading 2 on page 111 and complete the outline showing the organization of the essay. Write notes; do not copy whole sentences.

introductory paragraph	background information: thesis statement:
body paragraph 1	position 1 with supporting arguments and details:
body paragraph 2	position 2 with supporting arguments and details:
concluding paragraph	summary of both arguments: your opinion with reasons: prediction or recommendation:

WRITING TASK

> Should universities require students to take physical education classes? Discuss both sides and give your opinion.

PLAN

1 Look at the table you created in Exercise 4 in the Critical thinking section. Use the outline to plan your opinion essay.

introductory paragraph	background information: thesis statement:
body paragraph 1	position 1 with supporting arguments and details:
body paragraph 2	position 2 with supporting arguments and details:
concluding paragraph	summary of both arguments: your opinion with reasons: prediction or recommendation:

WRITE A FIRST DRAFT

2 Write a balanced opinion essay answering the question in the Writing task. Use the plan above to help you. Remember to include an introductory paragraph, two body paragraphs and a concluding paragraph.
Write 250–300 words.

REVISE

3 Use the Task checklist to review your essay for content and structure.

TASK CHECKLIST	✔
Does your introductory paragraph include background information and a thesis statement?	
Does your essay follow the structure provided?	
Do your arguments reflect both sides of the question?	
Does your concluding paragraph summarize the arguments and give your opinion?	

4 Make any necessary changes to your essay.

EDIT

5 Use the Language checklist to edit your essay for language errors.

LANGUAGE CHECKLIST	✔
Did you use a range of academic nouns and verbs?	
Did you use health and fitness collocations?	
Did you use opinion phrases or modals for stating your opinion?	
Did you use *to*, *in order to*, *so* and *so that* correctly to state a purpose?	
Did you use *but*, *however*, *although* and *on the other hand* to link contrasting sentences?	

6 Make any necessary changes to your essay.

OBJECTIVES REVIEW

1 Check your learning objectives for this unit. Write *3, 2* or *1* for each objective.

3 = very well   2 = well   1 = not so well

I can ...

watch and understand a video about the amount of sugar in
food and drinks. _____

make inferences. _____

support an argument. _____

use verb and noun forms. _____

state opinions. _____

state a purpose. _____

link contrasting sentences. _____

structure an essay (introductory, body and concluding paragraphs). _____

write a balanced opinion essay. _____

2 Use the *Unlock* Digital Workbook for more practice with this unit's learning objectives.

WORDLIST

active (adj) ⦿	junk food (n)	portion (n) ⦿
advertising campaign (n)	life expectancy (n)	recognize (v) ⦿
balanced diet (n)	moderate (adj) ⦿	reduce (v) ⦿
calories (n pl)	nutritional (adj) ⦿	regular exercise (n)
campaign (n) ⦿	nutritional value (n)	self-esteem (n)
educational programme (n)	obesity (n)	serious (adj) ⦿
heart disease (n)	physical activity (n)	serious illness (n)

⦿ = high-frequency words in the Cambridge Academic Corpus

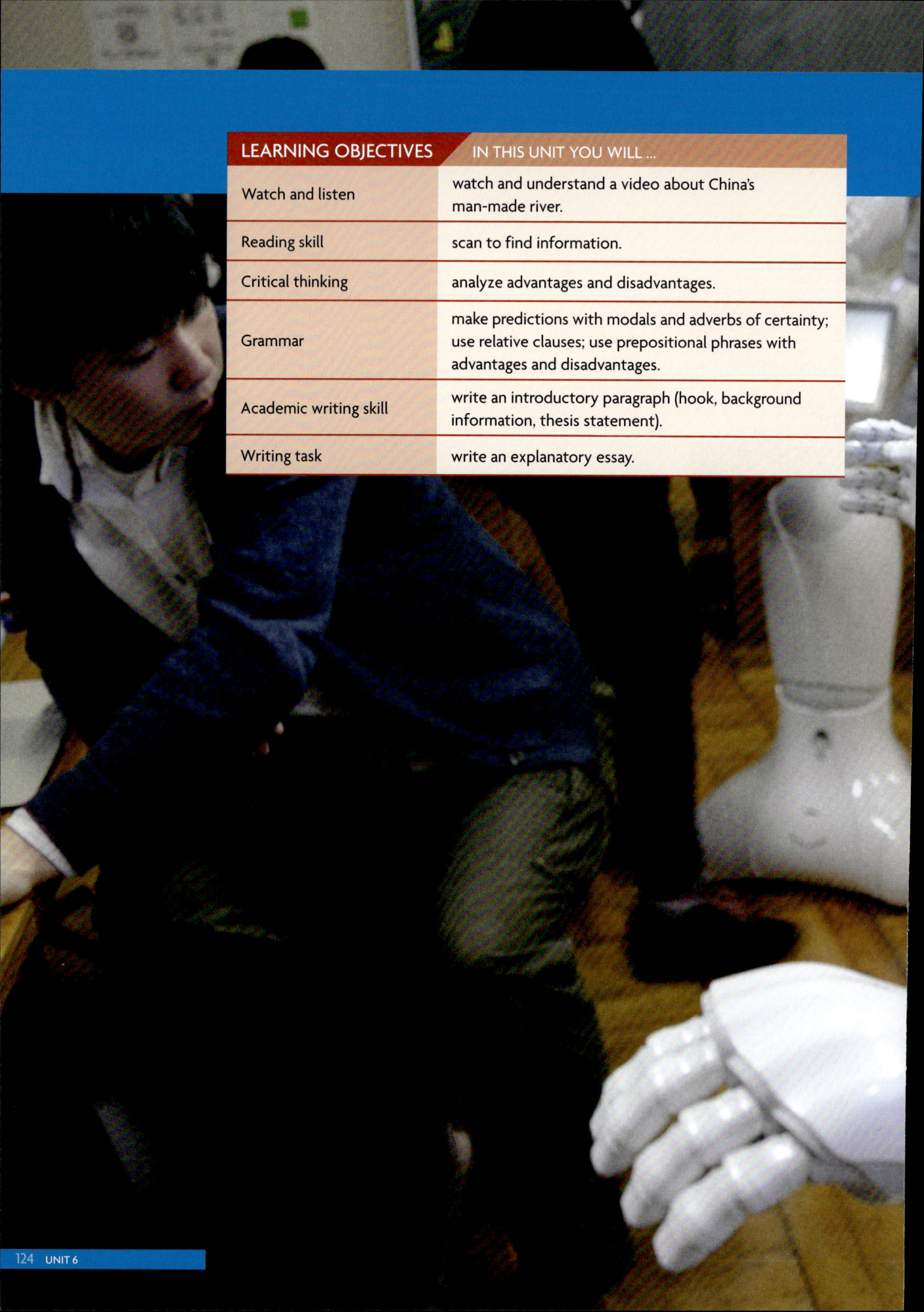

LEARNING OBJECTIVES	IN THIS UNIT YOU WILL ...
Watch and listen	watch and understand a video about China's man-made river.
Reading skill	scan to find information.
Critical thinking	analyze advantages and disadvantages.
Grammar	make predictions with modals and adverbs of certainty; use relative clauses; use prepositional phrases with advantages and disadvantages.
Academic writing skill	write an introductory paragraph (hook, background information, thesis statement).
Writing task	write an explanatory essay.

DISCOVERY AND INVENTION

UNIT 6

UNLOCK YOUR KNOWLEDGE

Work with a partner. Discuss the questions.

1 Look at the photo. What is happening? Will scenes like this become more common in the future? Explain your answer.
2 What do you think will happen in science and technology over the next ten years? What kinds of new inventions will there be? How will they help people? Will there be any disadvantages?
3 If you could invent one thing to help the world, what would it be? How would it help?

WATCH AND LISTEN

PREPARING TO WATCH

ACTIVATING YOUR KNOWLEDGE

1 You are going to watch a video about a river in China. Before you watch, work with a partner and discuss the questions.

1 What are some inventions to help us control our natural environment?
2 How does water get into your home?
3 How does water become clean enough to drink?

PREDICTING CONTENT USING VISUALS

2 Work with a partner. Look at the photos from the video and discuss the questions.

1 What do you think these people are building?
2 What problem could this project solve?

GLOSSARY

obstacle (n) something that blocks you so that movement or action is stopped or made more difficult

canal (n) a man-made river built for boats to travel along, or to take water where it is needed

frame (n) the basic part of a building, vehicle, piece of furniture, etc. that other parts are added onto

concrete (n) a hard material that is used in building and made by mixing sand, water, small stones and cement

crane (n) a large, usually tall machine used for lifting and moving heavy things

pump (n) a piece of equipment which pushes liquid or gas somewhere, especially through pipes or tubes

WHILE WATCHING

UNDERSTANDING MAIN IDEAS

3 ▶ Watch the video. Answer the questions.
1. Where do most of the people in China live? _____
2. What problem does the video say China has? _____
3. How is each section of the canal built? _____
4. Why does the crane operator have to be very careful?
   _____
5. When will the project be completed? _____
6. Who will the new canal help? _____

UNDERSTANDING DETAIL

4 ▶ Watch again. Correct the student notes.

1	Problem = people in north need food
2	Solution = build a lake
3	Length = 715 km
4	Weight of each concrete section = 12 tonnes
5	End of each section = 1 cm higher than other end
6	Finish date = 2020

DISCUSSION

5 Work in small groups. Discuss the questions.
1. Can you think of any other large engineering projects which have helped people to solve a problem? Discuss the problems and their engineering solutions and make a list.
2. Are there any problems in your city or country which engineering could solve, for example, the building of a new bridge or underground railway system? Discuss the problems and some possible solutions.
3. Imagine your group work for an international finance company. You want to support one of the projects in question 2. Discuss the strengths and weaknesses of each idea and decide which one to invest your money in.

READING

READING 1

PREPARING TO READ

UNDERSTANDING KEY VOCABULARY

1 Read the definitions and complete the sentences with the correct form of the words in bold.

> **essential** (adj) very important or necessary
> **harmful** (adj) able to hurt or damage
> **helpful** (adj) useful
> **illustrate** (v) to show the meaning or truth of something more clearly, especially by giving examples
> **pattern** (n) a set of lines, colours or shapes which repeat in a regular way
> **prevent** (v) to stop something from happening or stop someone from doing something
> **unlimited** (adj) without end or restriction

1 Before the invention of sunscreen, people had no way to protect themselves from the _____ rays of the sun.
2 Many cooks say that the food processor was a _____ invention because it saves a lot of preparation time in the kitchen.
3 Vaccines are a special group of medicines. They _____ illnesses from happening, rather than treating an illness we already have.
4 The planet Uranus has an interesting _____ of stripes, which is visible by viewing the planet with a telescope.
5 The human brain has an almost _____ memory capacity, far more than that of a computer.
6 If you want to be an engineer or a scientist, it's _____ that you have good qualifications in Science and Maths.
7 The engineer used diagrams to _____ his point about the mechanics of suspension bridges like the Golden Gate Bridge.

USING YOUR KNOWLEDGE

2 Work with a partner. Discuss the questions.

1 *Bio-* is a prefix which means 'life'. What words do you know that start with *bio-*?
2 Read the title and the first paragraph of the article on page 129. What do you think *mimicry* and *biomimicry* mean?
3 Can you think of any inventions which copy their shape or function from something in nature?

THE MAGIC OF MIMICRY

1 To *mimic* people means to copy their speech, dress or behaviour. In contrast, in science, *mimic* means copying ideas from nature or natural processes to solve problems or to create **helpful** products. The influence of this so-called *biomimicry* can be seen in a huge range of everyday products, from clothing to cars.

2 Perhaps the best-known example of biomimicry is Velcro®. It was invented in 1941 by a Swiss engineer called George de Mestral. One day, Mestral noticed the burdock seeds that stuck to his dog's hair. Under the microscope, he discovered that these seeds had hooks on them, so they stuck to loops on clothing or hair. Mestral copied this idea and created two strips of material: one with tiny hooks and the other with loose loops. When he put both strips together, they stuck like glue. However, unlike with glue, he could peel the strips apart and reattach them. Velcro® was initially unpopular with fashion companies, but after it was used by NASA to stop items from floating in space, it became popular with children's clothing companies. Today, it is used to fasten everything from lunch bags to shoes.

3 More recently, swimwear has also been influenced by nature. The Speedo Fastskin®, a controversial swimsuit, was seen at the Beijing Olympics in 2008 and worn by 28 of the 33 gold medal winners. The technology is based on the rough **patterns** on a shark's skin, which allow the shark to swim faster. A shark's skin also **prevents** bacteria from growing on it, so scientists are copying this surface to design cleaner hospitals.

4 For NASA, protecting astronauts' eyes from the sun's rays is very important, but protecting their eyes from other dangerous radiation is also **essential**. Scientists studied how eagles and falcons clearly recognize their prey. Scientists discovered that the birds have yellow oil in their eyes, which filters out **harmful** radiation and allows them to see very clearly. NASA copied this oil, and it is now used by astronauts and pilots in Eagle Eyes® glasses. In addition to protecting eyes from dangerous rays, these sunglasses also improve vision in different weather conditions such as fog, sunlight or just normal light.

5 In another example of biomimicry, Mercedes-Benz developed a concept car which was based on the shape of the tropical boxfish. Opinions were divided about the car's appearance, but the engineers at Mercedes-Benz chose to copy the boxfish skeleton to make their Bionic Car because of its strength and low weight. The boxfish's bony body protects the animal's insides from injury in the same way that a car needs to protect the people inside it. This shape also meant that the car had less air resistance and therefore used less fuel.

6 As these examples **illustrate**, biomimicry appears to have an **unlimited** number of applications. It will be interesting to see which problems nature helps us solve in the future.

WHILE READING

READING FOR MAIN IDEAS

3 Read the article and choose the sentence which best summarizes the main idea of the article.

a Though sharks can be dangerous, their skin is useful.
b In the future, nature can help us solve many important problems.
c Many useful products have been designed using biomimicry.
d Many useful discoveries have been made by accident.

> **SKILLS**
>
> ### Scanning to find information
> Scanning means reading for specific information. When you scan a text, do not read every word. Look for key words that help you understand what the text is about and identify specific information. For example, look for names, numbers, pronouns or groups of words related to the same topic/theme (e.g. words related to engineering, animals, etc.).

SCANNING TO FIND INFORMATION

4 Scan the magazine article on page 129 quickly to answer the questions.

1 Which products are mentioned in the article?
 _____
2 Which plants or animals were copied to produce these products?
 _____

ANNOTATING

5 Read the article to find the answers to the questions and annotate the text as you read. Look at page 85 for what to annotate. Write summary notes in the margin.

1 Which two features of Velcro® make the strips stick together?
2 What are some uses of Velcro®?
3 What product mimics a shark's skin?
4 What does a shark's skin allow the shark to do?
5 Whose eyes did NASA want to protect from dangerous radiation?
6 What special feature of an eagle's eyes was copied to make sunglasses?
7 What feature does the Bionic Car copy that allows it to save fuel?

READING BETWEEN THE LINES

MAKING INFERENCES

6 Work with a partner. Answer the questions.

1 Why do you think Velcro® became popular with children's clothing companies?
 _____

2 Why do you think the Speedo Fastskin® swimsuit was controversial during the Beijing Olympics?
 _____

3 Why do people have different opinions about the Bionic Car?
 _____

DISCUSSION

7 Work with a partner. Discuss the questions.

1 Do you think biomimicry will be more common in the future? Why / Why not?
2 What are the advantages of copying from nature? Can you think of any disadvantages?

READING 2

PREPARING TO READ

UNDERSTANDING KEY VOCABULARY

1 You are going to read an article about technology in the future. Before you read the article, read the definitions below. Complete the sentences with the correct form of the words in bold.

> **artificial** (adj) made by people, not in nature
> **break down** (phr v) to stop working, e.g. a machine
> **electronic** (adj) sent or accessed by a computer or similar machine
> **equipment** (n) things that are used for a particular activity or purpose
> **movement** (n) a change of position or place
> **object** (n) a thing you can see or touch that is not alive
> **personal** (adj) belonging to, or used by, just one person
> **three-dimensional** (adj) not flat; having depth, length and width; 3D

1 New technology can bring great advantages, but the cost of buying new _____ can be very high.
2 Social media sites allow us to choose what we see and who we communicate with online. Each person's media profile is _____ and is different from anyone else's.
3 You don't need a paper ticket because I've got an _____ one on my phone.
4 _____ films are more realistic than normal films. Everything on the screen looks like real life.
5 Hi-tech robots used in industry have arms that are capable of _____ in every direction.
6 Since mobile phones were invented, it has been much easier for people to get help if their car _____ on the road.
7 Microscopes allow us to see _____ that are too small to see with our eyes.
8 _____ legs have become so advanced that people who use them can run marathons and climb mountains.

USING YOUR KNOWLEDGE

2 Work with a partner. Answer the questions.

1 Do you think flying cars will be a reality someday? Why / Why not?
_____
_____

2 What is a 3D printer? What is it used for?
_____
_____

3 How can robots help people who are missing arms or legs?
_____
_____

WHILE READING

SCANNING TO FIND INFORMATION

3 Scan the article on page 133 to answer the questions. Look for the bold phrases in the questions.

1 Which paragraph describes a **robot suit**? _____
2 Which paragraph describes a **flying car**? _____
3 Which paragraph describes a **3D printer**? _____

READING FOR MAIN IDEAS

4 Read the article and complete the table with the advantages and disadvantages of each invention.

a The equipment costs a lot of money.
b We could avoid speeding tickets.
c It could help people walk again.
d Mechanical failure might be a big problem.
e There are problems with cost and battery life.
f We could make our own plastic products.

invention	advantages	disadvantages
1 flying car		
2 3D printing		
3 robot suit		

THE WORLD OF TOMORROW

1 What will the world of the next generation look like? And the generations after that? Many people today are confident that technology is going to help solve some of the most challenging problems we have on Earth today, such as global warming and hunger. Other people are worried that while new technology may solve old problems, it may also create new ones. No technology is perfect; each innovation has advantages and disadvantages, as these three examples illustrate.

2 When we dream about the future, many of us like to think that we will be able to exit our garages and take to the skies in our own **personal** flying car. The advantages are obvious. This technology would allow total freedom of **movement**. We could fly at 480 km per hour, avoiding traffic lights, busy roads and speeding tickets. However, some people believe there will be problems with traffic control. If the cars become popular, there is likely to be air traffic congestion. Another big problem is mechanical failure. What will happen if the cars **break down**? These are problems we must expect if flying cars become a reality.

3 **Three-dimensional** printing is another new technology with exciting possibilities for the future. 3D printers are used to build an **object** with liquid plastic. They build the object layer by layer until it is complete. Car companies already use 3D printers to make life-size models of car parts, and medical companies use the technology to make **artificial** body parts, such as ears. Before long, it might be possible to see a product on a website and then download it to your 3D printer at home. As we move into the future, 3D printing will revolutionize the way we shop, the way we manufacture and the way we treat sick people. The downside is that such **equipment** will be extremely expensive.

4 Finally, imagine having your own Iron Man suit. Several companies are trying to build a practical robot *exoskeleton*. This is an **electronic** suit with robot arms and legs which follows the wearer's movements. Exoskeletons allow you to lift heavy objects, walk long distances and even punch through walls! There are obvious military advantages for this technology, but there are also benefits for rescue workers or people with disabilities. The suit might help people walk again after disease or injury. However, one disadvantage at the moment is cost. Even a simple exoskeleton can cost hundreds of thousands of pounds. Another problem is battery life. A heavy suit like this needs a lot of power, and battery life is short. However, these problems will no doubt be solved as lightweight plastic suits become available.

5 Looking ahead, it is not difficult imagine a future when we will be able to fly to work, print out a new pair of shoes or lift a car above our heads. Although there are some problems to solve before all of this is possible, we can certainly dream of a world where technology makes life easier and safer for millions of people.

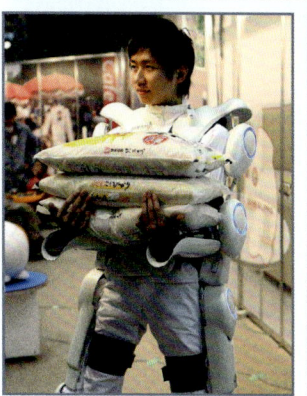

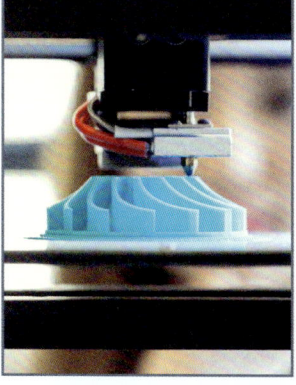

READING FOR DETAIL

5 Read the article again and write *T* (true), *F* (false) or *DNS* (does not say) next to the statements. Then, correct the false statements.

_____ 1 Flying cars will allow us to avoid traffic congestion on the roads.
_____

_____ 2 Mechanical failure will not be a problem for flying cars.
_____

_____ 3 We might be able to print things like hearts or lungs in the future.
_____

_____ 4 3D printing was invented in 1984.
_____

_____ 5 Car companies make model car parts with 3D printers.
_____

_____ 6 Robot suits are heavy objects.
_____

_____ 7 The battery life of a robot suit is long at the moment.
_____

READING BETWEEN THE LINES

MAKING INFERENCES

6 Work with a partner. Answer the questions.

1 Why is mechanical failure a possible problem in a flying car?
_____

2 Why will flying cars cause traffic congestion instead of reducing it?
_____

3 What do you think could be some of the medical benefits of robot suits?
_____

4 What could be some of the reasons robotic exoskeletons are expensive?
_____

DISCUSSION

SYNTHESIZING

7 Work with a partner. Use ideas from Reading 1 and Reading 2 to answer the following questions.

1 Consider all the inventions in Reading 1 and Reading 2. Imagine the year is 2035. Which inventions do you think you will use regularly? Why?

2 Think of some machines or devices you use every day. Which ones will probably not exist in 2035 because something better has replaced them?

LANGUAGE DEVELOPMENT

MAKING PREDICTIONS WITH MODALS AND ADVERBS OF CERTAINTY

> Use the modals *will, could* and *won't* with an adverb of certainty (*definitely, probably,* etc.) before the main verb to talk about future predictions. For example:
>
> 100% = *will definitely*
> Cars **will definitely** become more efficient in the future.
>
> 90% = *will probably*
> The next generation **will probably** use more digital devices.
>
> 50% = *could possibly*
> We **could possibly** see humans walking on Mars soon.
>
> 20% = *probably won't*
> We **probably won't** have flying cars.
>
> 0% = *definitely won't*
> We **definitely won't** be travelling to the stars.

1 Complete the sentences about the future using modal and adverb phrases with the meaning in brackets.

1 In years to come, biofuels _____ become more important. (100%)
2 Genetic modification _____ be very controversial before the end of the decade. (20%)
3 In the near future, electronic human implants _____ become very common. (90%)
4 Biomimicry _____ be a growing industry before too long. (90%)
5 Self-driving cars _____ be everyday products within the next ten years. (100%)
6 People _____ own Iron Man suits within the next few years. (0%)
7 By 2035, many people _____ have a 3D printer in their homes. (50%)

2 Look again at Exercise 1 and underline the phrases which refer to future time.

PREFIXES

VOCABULARY

A prefix is a group of letters which goes at the start of a word to make a new word with a different meaning. Each prefix has a specific meaning.

sub (prefix meaning 'under') + *marine* (word related to water) = a kind of boat which goes under the water

Understanding the meaning of prefixes can help you guess the general meaning of difficult academic or technical words.

3 Look at these prefixes, their meanings and the examples. Then, add your own examples to the table. Use a dictionary to help you.

prefix	meaning	example
de-	become less, go down	decrease, _____ , _____
dis-	opposite	disagree, _____ , _____
en-	cause	enable, _____ , _____
pre-	before	prevent, _____ , _____
re-	again	rebuild, _____ , _____
trans-	across, through	transport, _____ , _____
un-	remove, not	unlikely, _____ , _____

4 Compare the pairs of sentences using the table above. Do the sentences have the same or opposite meanings? Write *S* (the same) or *O* (opposite).

1 Flying cars are **unsafe**.
  Flying cars are dangerous. ____
2 We have to **rethink** the way we use technology.
  We have to think again about how we use technology. ____
3 Genetic engineering **dehumanizes** us.
  Genetic engineering makes us more human. ____
4 Can this software **translate** a document from French to English?
  Can this software change the language of a document from French to English? ____
5 Seat belts in cars **prevent** many injuries and deaths.
  Seat belts cause many injuries and deaths. ____
6 This laboratory is very **disorganized**.
  This laboratory is neat. ____
7 The font on your presentation is too small. Can you **enlarge** it?
  Can you make it bigger? ____

5 Work with a partner. Choose words from the table above and make five predictions about new technology. Then, compare your ideas.

WRITING

CRITICAL THINKING

At the end of this unit, you will write an explanatory essay. Look at this unit's writing task below.

> Choose a new area of technology or invention and discuss its advantages and disadvantages.

Analyzing advantages and disadvantages

A common way of explaining a topic is to discuss its advantages (benefits or positive aspects) and disadvantages (problems or negative aspects). When planning an essay organized in this way, you may want to use a kind of graphic organizer called a T-chart, which is useful for examining two sides or aspects of a topic. Look at the example.

invention: tablet computers	
advantages	disadvantages
lightweight portable fast start-up	no physical keyboard too small for working on multiple documents uncomfortable to use for long periods of time

1 Look back at Reading 2 on page 133 and choose one invention from the reading. Then, complete the T-chart with its advantages and disadvantages.

UNDERSTAND

invention: _____	
advantages	disadvantages

REMEMBER

2 Work with a partner. Brainstorm recent inventions in each area of technology below. You could also do an internet search for 'best recent inventions in …'.

areas of technology	inventions
medicine	CT scanner, insulin pump,
home	
space	
transport	
entertainment	
computers	
agriculture	

APPLY

3 Choose one of the inventions from your table in Exercise 2. Fill in the T-chart with advantages and disadvantages of this invention.

invention: _____	
advantages	disadvantages

ANALYZE

4 Work with a partner. Explain why you think the invention you chose will / will not be around ten years from now.

GRAMMAR FOR WRITING

RELATIVE CLAUSES

Use *relative clauses* to give more information about a noun without starting a new sentence. There are two kinds of relative clauses: defining and non-defining. Defining relative clauses give essential information about the noun. In contrast, non-defining relative clauses give extra, non-essential information about the noun. These clauses can be removed from the sentence, but the key information about the noun will still be clear. Non-defining relative clauses have commas before and sometimes after them. Defining relative clauses do not.

defining clauses	
use *who* or *that* for people and *which* or *that* for things	Velcro® has a unique **structure**. It allows two strips to stick together. → Velcro® has a unique structure **which / that** allows two strips to stick together.
non-defining clauses	
use *who* for people and *which* for things	Velcro® was invented in 1941 by George de Mestral. **George de Mestral** saw the seeds on his dog's hair. → Velcro® was invented in 1941 by George de Mestral, **who** saw the seeds on his dog's hair.

1 Complete the sentences with *who*, *which* or *that*. Then, underline the relative clauses and write D (defining) or N (non-defining).

1 The Speedo Fastskin® swimsuit uses a technology _____ is based on the rough patterns on a shark's skin. _____
2 Scientists discovered that eagles and falcons have oil over their eyes. The oil, _____ filters out harmful radiation, allows them to see very clearly. _____
3 Robotic exoskeletons will be useful for rescue workers like firefighters, _____ often have to lift people out of burning buildings or cars. _____
4 People _____ are unable to walk may be able to walk with the help of a robotic suit. _____
5 3D printing, _____ makes it possible to build objects using layers of liquid plastic, may allow shoppers to see a product online and then download it to their printer at home. _____

2 Join each pair of sentences to make one sentence with a relative clause. Add commas if necessary.

1 Scientists have already developed new robots. New robots are able to do dangerous work.
   _____

2 There is a great deal of technology to help elderly people. Elderly people may have trouble doing some tasks by themselves.
   _____

3 There is a huge amount of new investment in biofuels. Biofuels are cleaner and more sustainable than fossil fuels.
   _____

4 The Bionic Car has a special design. A special design makes it more fuel efficient.
   _____

5 Important research is being done by scientists at the University of Cambridge. Scientists at the University of Cambridge hope to publish their results next year.
   _____

PREPOSITIONAL PHRASES WITH ADVANTAGES AND DISADVANTAGES

> A *prepositional phrase* consists of a preposition, a noun and, in many cases, a noun modifier (a word which changes a noun, such as an adjective). For example:
>
> at home   by the red door
> in the morning   under the living-room rug
>
> Writers often use prepositional phrases at the start of a new sentence to introduce the advantages and disadvantages of a subject.
>
> An **advantage of** 3D printing is that you can make products anywhere.
> One of the main **problems with** 3D printing is that it's still very expensive.

3 Complete the table with the phrases in bold.

1 The main **advantage of** … is …
2 The main **disadvantage of** … is …
3 The main **worry about** … is …
4 One **point against** … is …
5 One **good thing about** … is …
6 One **bad thing about** … is …
7 A real **benefit of** … is …
8 The main **argument in favour of** … is …
9 The main **argument against** … is …
10 The **problem with** … is …

positive arguments	negative arguments

4 Choose a negative or positive phrase from Exercise 3 to complete each sentence. More than one answer is possible.

1 _____ robots is that they can do dangerous or boring jobs instead of humans.
2 _____ genetic engineering is that the new plant species may change human DNA.
3 _____ medical imaging is that you can see clearly inside patients' bodies.
4 _____ robots is that they take jobs away from people.
5 _____ flying cars is that they could crash, causing terrible accidents.

ACADEMIC WRITING SKILLS

WRITING AN INTRODUCTORY PARAGRAPH

The first, or introductory, paragraph of an essay usually has three parts:
- a hook
- background information
- a thesis statement

The **hook** is a statement, definition or question at the beginning of the paragraph. Its purpose is to get the reader interested in the topic so he or she will want to keep reading. A good hook can be an interesting question, a surprising fact or statistic, a request to the reader to imagine a situation, a definition, something another person said, etc. For example:

In 2014, Americans spent 6.9 billion hours sitting in traffic. Imagine what we could do with all that time if we did not need to commute.

Many nations are in danger of running out of water. However, a company has invented a machine which turns water from the air into water you can drink.

Background information helps readers understand the essay. Background information can include an explanation of words or phrases, historical information, data and statistics or a general explanation of the topic.

This is an electronic suit with robot arms and legs which follows the wearer's movements.

The **thesis statement** is usually the last sentence of the introduction. It tells the reader how the essay will be developed. Often a thesis statement has two parts: a topic and a point of view. For example:

   topic   point of view

<u>Flying cars</u> may reduce congestion on the ground, but they may create additional problems, such as congestion in the air and pollution.

This thesis statement informs the reader that the topic, flying cars, will be followed by both advantages and disadvantages of flying cars.

1 Read the first paragraph of the article on page 129 again. Answer the questions.

1 What is the hook? Does it get your attention? If so, how?

2 What kind of background information does the paragraph include?

3 According to the thesis statement, what is the topic of the article? What is the point of view? How many paragraphs will the body of the article probably have? What will each paragraph probably discuss?

2 Now read the introductory paragraph to 'The world of tomorrow' on page 133 again. Answer the questions.

1 What is the hook? Does it get your attention?
___

2 What kind of background information does the paragraph include?
___

3 According to the thesis statement, what is the topic of the article? What is the point of view? How many paragraphs will the body of the article probably have? What will each paragraph probably discuss?
___
___

4 Which of the two introductions makes you more interested as a reader? Why?
___

WRITING TASK

▎Choose a new area of technology or invention and discuss its advantages and disadvantages.

PLAN

1 Look at the table you created in Exercise 3 in the Critical thinking section.

2 Plan your essay's introductory paragraph. Write notes on the following parts of the introduction.

Hook:
___

Background information:
___

Thesis statement:
___

3 Create an outline for the body of your essay. How many paragraphs will it have? Make sure the number of paragraphs matches the point of view in your thesis statement. Be sure to include advantages and disadvantages.
___
___
___
___
___
___
___

4 Plan your concluding paragraph. It should repeat your thesis statement and make a prediction about the future.

_____
_____

5 Use the Task checklist below as you prepare your essay.

WRITE A FIRST DRAFT

6 Write the first draft of your essay using your essay plan. Write 250–300 words.

REVISE

7 Use the Task checklist to review your essay for content and structure.

TASK CHECKLIST	✔
Did you write about advantages and disadvantages?	
Did you include an introductory paragraph that has a hook, background information and a thesis statement?	
Does the number of paragraphs in the body match the point of view in the thesis statement?	
Do the main body paragraphs have a topic sentence, supporting sentences and a concluding sentence?	
Does the concluding paragraph repeat the thesis statement and make a prediction about the future?	

8 Make any necessary changes to your essay.

EDIT

9 Use the Language checklist to edit your essay for language errors.

LANGUAGE CHECKLIST	✔
Did you use modals and adverbs of certainty to make predictions about the future?	
Did you use *who*, *that* and *which* correctly in sentences with relative clauses? Did you use commas correctly?	
Did you introduce advantages and disadvantages with prepositional phrases?	

10 Make any necessary changes to your essay.

OBJECTIVES REVIEW

1 Check your learning objectives for this unit. Write *3, 2* or *1* for each objective.

3 = very well   2 = well   1 = not so well

I can ...

watch and understand a video about China's man-made river. _____

scan to find information. _____

analyze advantages and disadvantages. _____

make predictions with modals and adverbs of certainty. _____

use relative clauses. _____

use prepositional phrases with advantages and disadvantages. _____

write an introductory paragraph (hook, background information, thesis statement). _____

write an explanatory essay. _____

2 Use the *Unlock* Digital Workbook for more practice with this unit's learning objectives.

WORDLIST

artificial (adj) ⊙	essential (adj) ⊙	personal (adj) ⊙
break down (phr v)	harmful (adj) ⊙	prevent (v) ⊙
dehumanize (v)	helpful (adj) ⊙	rethink (v)
disorganized (adj)	illustrate (v) ⊙	three-dimensional (adj) ⊙
electronic (adj) ⊙	movement (n) ⊙	translate (v) ⊙
enlarge (v)	object (n) ⊙	unlimited (adj)
equipment (n) ⊙	pattern (n) ⊙	unsafe (adj)

⊙ = high-frequency words in the Cambridge Academic Corpus

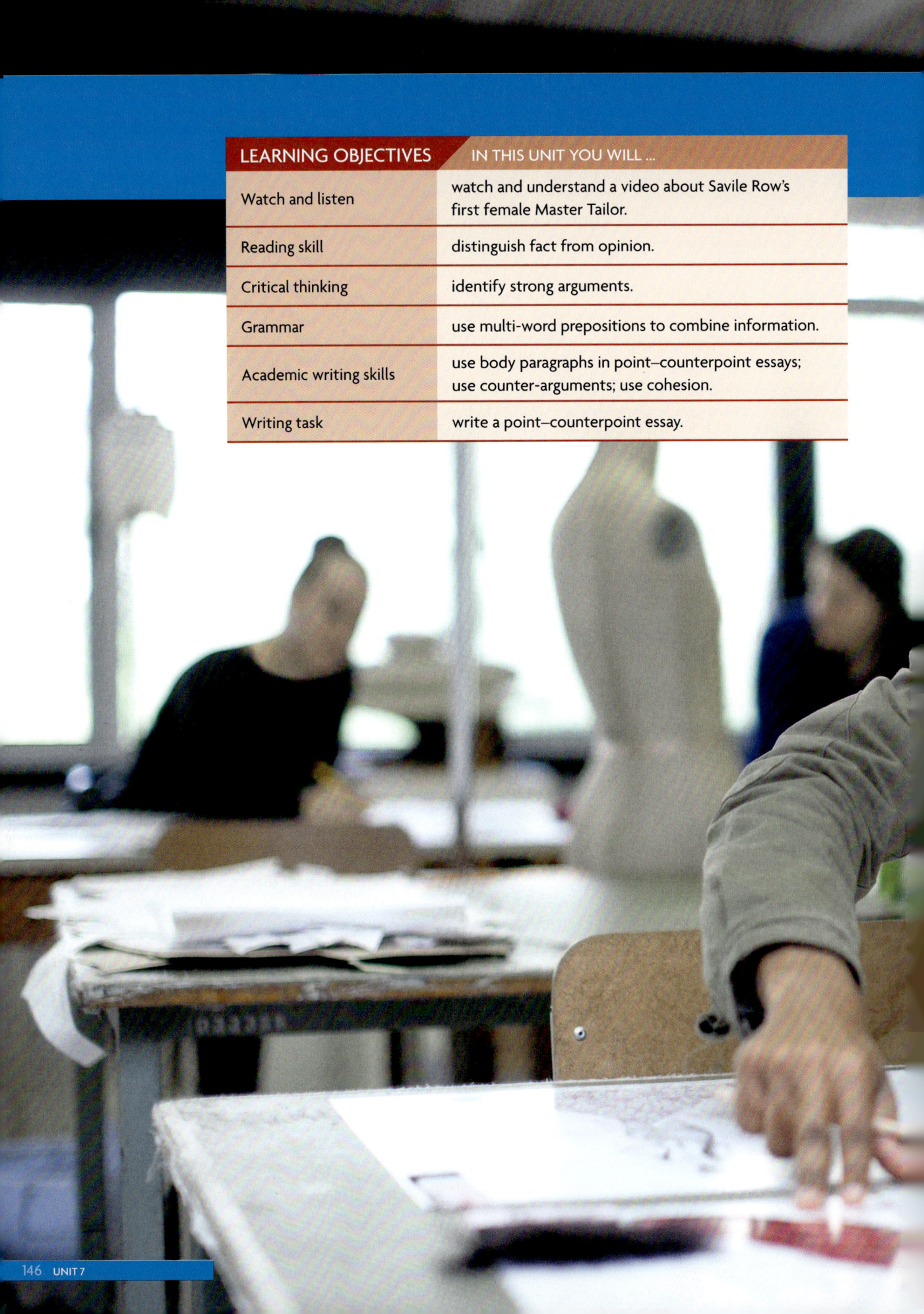

LEARNING OBJECTIVES	IN THIS UNIT YOU WILL ...
Watch and listen	watch and understand a video about Savile Row's first female Master Tailor.
Reading skill	distinguish fact from opinion.
Critical thinking	identify strong arguments.
Grammar	use multi-word prepositions to combine information.
Academic writing skills	use body paragraphs in point–counterpoint essays; use counter-arguments; use cohesion.
Writing task	write a point–counterpoint essay.

FASHION

UNIT 7

UNLOCK YOUR KNOWLEDGE

Work with a partner. Discuss the questions.

1 Look at the photo. What is the man doing? Do you think this is important work? Why / Why not?
2 Why do people buy designer clothing?
3 Do you prefer designer clothing or clothes that are not designer? Why / Why not?
4 Are stores which sell cheap clothes popular in your country? Why / Why not?

WATCH AND LISTEN

PREPARING TO WATCH

ACTIVATING YOUR KNOWLEDGE

1 Work with a partner. Look at the different places in the box where clothes can be made. Discuss the questions about each place.

> at home   in a factory   in a tailor's shop

1 What kinds of clothes are often made in this place? How fashionable do you think the clothes made here are? Why?
2 Do you think the clothes are made by hand or machine? Why?
3 How long do you think it takes to make the clothes? What quality do you think they will be? How well will the clothes fit? Why?
4 Do you think men, women or both men and women make the clothes in these places? Why?

PREDICTING CONTENT USING VISUALS

2 Work with a partner. You are going to watch a video about someone who works in fashion. Before you watch, look at the pictures and discuss the questions.

1 What city do you think this is? What do you think the shops on this street sell?
2 Do you think that the people who shop here are mostly men, women or a mix? Why?
3 What is the woman's job? Do you think she owns the business she works at or not? Why?

> **GLOSSARY**
>
> **tailor** (n) a person whose job it is to make or mend clothes, especially men's clothes
>
> **master tailor** (n) the head tailor of a company who teaches other, less experienced tailors
>
> **prominent position** (n phr) important job
>
> **apprentice** (n) a person who is learning a job by working for someone who already has skills and experience
>
> **values/principles** (n pl) what you believe is the right and wrong way to do things; what you believe is important in life

WHILE WATCHING

3 ▶ Watch the video. Then answer the questions.

1 What is the street seen in the video (Savile Row) famous for?
   _____
2 Who is Kathryn Sargent? Why is she important? _____
3 What is changing on Savile Row? _____

4 ▶ Watch again. Write *T* (true) or *F* (false) next to the statements. Then, correct the false statements.

_____ 1 A Savile Row suit can take 50 hours or more to make.
   _____
_____ 2 Women only recently started working on Savile Row.
   _____
_____ 3 Kathryn Sargent owns her own business.
   _____
_____ 4 Last year, more than 65% of new tailors were male.
   _____
_____ 5 Kathryn learnt how to make suits on Savile Row.
   _____
_____ 6 Kathryn believes in different ideas to the other Savile Row tailors.
   _____

5 ▶ Watch again. Complete the gaps with words from the video. Then, work with a partner and discuss the meaning of the words and phrases in bold.

1 Until now, no woman has **made it to the top** on Savile Row and _____ .
2 It's **a sign of the times** really. There are far more _____ now.
3 Just **behind the scenes**, there have always been women present within the workrooms on Savile Row, but now there are more women _____ within the trade.
4 As I said, _____ ; it's a very small **network**.

DISCUSSION

6 Work in small groups. Discuss the questions.

1 How is Kathryn Sargent's work different from work women have done on Savile Row in the past? What different tasks do you think she does? What could be the reasons for these differences?
2 Do you think other parts of the fashion industry, such as designer fashions and high street brands, have traditionally had different jobs for men and women? Why?
3 Do you think that Savile Row is likely to have an equal number of male and female tailors in the future? Why / Why not?

UNDERSTANDING MAIN IDEAS

UNDERSTANDING DETAIL

WORKING OUT MEANING FROM CONTEXT

READING

READING 1

PREPARING TO READ

UNDERSTANDING KEY VOCABULARY

1 You are going to read an article about fashion. Before you read the article, read the sentences (1–7) and write the correct form of the words in bold next to the definitions (a–g).

1 When you shop for clothes, do you search for specific **brands**, or do you just buy what you like?
2 When a clothing company increases its prices, it is common for the company's sales **volume** to fall.
3 Everyone was talking about the new designer **collections** at the spring fashion show in Milan.
4 This **season** you can expect to see lots of clothes in bright colours in the shops.
5 **Cotton** clothes are cool and soft, and they are great for the summer.
6 These days, many clothing companies **manufacture** their clothes in Vietnam, Cambodia or other countries in Southeast Asia.
7 New companies have to **invest** millions of pounds in building factories and training employees.

a _____ (n) a time of year when particular things happen
b _____ (v) to make goods in a large quantity in a factory
c _____ (n) amount of something, especially when it is large
d _____ (n) a group of new clothes produced by a fashion company
e _____ (n) a plant used for making cloth, or the fabric made from the plant
f _____ (v) to use money for the purpose of making a profit, for example, by building a factory
g _____ (n) the name of a product, or group of products, made by a company

USING YOUR KNOWLEDGE

2 Work with a partner. Answer the questions.

1 What do you think the term *fast fashion* means?
   _____
2 How often do fashions tend to change?
   _____
3 If fashion designers changed fashions every month, what effect would this have on shoppers? On the clothing industry?
   _____

3 Read the article on page 151 and check your answers.

Is *fast fashion* taking over?

1. The fashion industry has changed significantly in recent years. Traditionally, fashion retailers[1] created two clothing **collections** per year, called **seasons**. Each season was a collection of clothes for spring/summer or autumn/winter. Nowadays, in contrast, they can design and **manufacture** clothes in as little as four weeks. *Fast fashion* means that the latest designs shown at the fashion shows in Paris, London, New York and Milan can be copied and sold in shopping malls within a month. A typical fast-fashion retailer can stock 10,000 designs annually, compared with 2,000 for its high-fashion competitors. The largest fast-fashion retailers have annual sales in the billions of euros.

2. The advantages of rapidly changing fashions are clear. Shortening the life cycle of a product means that if a design doesn't sell well within a week, it is taken out of the shops and replaced with a new one. This is good for manufacturers as it means a greater **volume** of sales. It is also good for customers, who can keep up with fast-moving trends cheaply and who can enjoy finding something new every time they visit the shop.

3. However, there are also a number of disadvantages to the fast-fashion approach. Perhaps the biggest concern is the impact of wasted clothes on the environment. The low cost of most fast fashion enables shoppers to buy several new sets of clothes each season instead of wearing the same outfits year after year. This means that a huge amount of clothing is thrown away. Furthermore, with fashions changing so quickly, **cotton** growers need to produce more cotton more cheaply, and that means using more pesticides and chemicals. A third problem is the theft of ideas. Fashion houses **invest** a lot of time and money in new designs, only to see these ideas stolen and copied by fast-fashion companies.

4. Fast fashion rests at one end of the fashion scale. At the other end is high-end designer clothing, where major changes are also happening. At the same time as fast fashion is becoming more and more popular, wealthy consumers worldwide are buying more and more expensive, luxury **brands**. Many wealthy customers buy designer clothes just to show that they can afford them, but others choose luxury brands for their quality, saying that they will last longer. They have a point. As they last longer, expensive designer clothes are more environmentally friendly.

5. In short, these days it seems that the fashion industry is changing almost as fast as the fashion it produces – but what do you think? We would like to hear your comments about the fashion industry today.

Comments
6 comments

Carmen — Reply
I'd love to have the money to buy designer clothes, but I have to buy cheaper products because I don't have much money. I'm sure the quality is not as good as clothes with designer labels.
👍 Like 14

Ahmet — Reply
Designer fashion is a waste of money. Wearing brand names is just free advertising for that company, and I don't think the quality is any different.
👍 Like 13

[1]**retailer** (n) someone who sells products to people

Jasmine — Reply

Great article!
I love fast fashion! I enjoy looking good and having lots of clothes. Fast fashion allows me to buy lots of clothes really cheaply. Why should I feel bad about throwing away cheap clothes when they go out of fashion? I can just go out and get more.

👍 Like 0

Ben — Reply
Response to Jasmine
Your attitude seems kind of selfish, Jasmine! What about the environment? Don't you think it's wrong to waste all those clothes? At least give the clothes to charity if you don't want them anymore.

👍 Like 7

Sara — Reply

Style is important to me. I study fashion at college and I would never buy fast fashion. I don't want to look like everyone else. I prefer to buy second-hand clothes because older clothes were designed to last. I have my own style. I don't need to copy Paris or Milan.

👍 Like 11

Fatima — Reply

I can understand why people like fast fashion, but I prefer to pay for quality, and if the shop has environmentally friendly clothes then that is perfect. I agree with Ben: we need to care for the planet; otherwise, our children won't have a planet to live on. I would rather pay more and know I'm helping to protect the Earth.

👍 Like 31

WHILE READING

READING FOR MAIN IDEAS

4 Read the article again and number the main ideas in the order that they are mentioned. One of the ideas is not mentioned. Remember that you can annotate the article as you read.

a designer clothing _____
b advantages of fast fashion _____
c fast-fashion shows _____
d the definition of *fast fashion* __1__
e disadvantages of fast fashion _____

5 Look at the article again and correct the factual mistakes in the sentences. The first one has been done for you as an example.

1 Traditional fashion retailers annually produce 10,000 designs.
   Traditional fashion retailers annually produce 2,000 designs.
2 High-end fashion designs that are unpopular are withdrawn in less than a week.
   _____
3 Traditional fashion is good for the manufacturer because of the greater volume of sales.
   _____
4 The biggest problem with fast fashion is the theft of ideas.
   _____
5 Cotton growers need to produce more, so they have to use fewer chemicals.
   _____
6 Designer clothing is popular with poorer shoppers.
   _____

READING FOR DETAIL

READING BETWEEN THE LINES

6 Look at the comments about the article on pages 151–152 and answer the questions.

1 Who is against designer fashion? _____
2 Who would like to buy more expensive clothes? _____
3 Who doesn't like to follow fashion trends? _____
4 Who has the most likes? Why?
   _____
5 Who has the fewest likes? Why?
   _____

MAKING INFERENCES

DISCUSSION

7 Work with a partner. Discuss the questions.

1 Do you have any fast-fashion clothing shops in your country? If so, do you ever shop at them? How often? What do you buy?
2 Which comment from the reading do you agree with the most? Why?
3 Which group of people do you think fashion is more important to? Younger or older people? Men or women? Explain your answer.

READING 2

PREPARING TO READ

UNDERSTANDING KEY VOCABULARY

1 Read the definitions and complete the sentences with the correct form of the words in bold.

> **conditions** (n pl) the physical environment where people live or work
> **import** (v) to buy a product from another country and bring it into your country
> **multinational** (adj) referring to a business or company that has offices, shops or factories in several countries
> **offshore** (adj) located in another country
> **outsource** (v) to have work done by another company, often in another country, rather than in your own company
> **textile** (n) cloth or fabric that is made by crossing threads under and over each other (by hand or machine)
> **wage** (n) money that people earn for working

1 Some _____ companies are so big that they have offices in more than a hundred countries.
2 Designers at famous fashion houses can earn high _____ .
3 The workers at that factory are well-paid, and their working _____ are safe and comfortable.
4 Scotland is famous for producing beautiful wool _____ , which are often used to make a traditional item of men's clothing called a kilt.
5 At one time, the company made all its products in the United States. In recent years, however, it decided to _____ its production to Singapore.
6 Many manufacturers do large parts of their production in _____ factories because materials and labour are cheaper in other countries.
7 We _____ fabric from China, then we sew and finish the shirts here.

USING YOUR KNOWLEDGE

2 Work with a partner. Discuss the questions.
1 Why do some companies outsource their production to other countries?
2 What are the benefits for a country when a multinational company moves its production there?
3 Are there any disadvantages for workers when multinational companies base their factories in their countries?

OFFSHORE PRODUCTION

1 The world's consumption of fashion is huge. To give just one example, the European Union **imported** almost €29 billion worth of clothing in 2015. As consumption has risen, prices have fallen. Today, a hand-finished shirt may cost as little as five euros. To make clothes at these low prices, companies have to keep costs down. One way they do this is by using **offshore** production. Large **multinational** companies **outsource** their production to developing countries like Egypt or Cambodia, where workers are paid much less than in developed countries. Supporters of outsourcing claim that it helps local economies, but I believe it is harmful for two main reasons.

2 Some experts, like the economist David Schneider, say that outsourcing benefits local economies by providing jobs at higher **wages** than local workers can make by working in agriculture. Supporters also point out that people in developing countries often line up to take jobs in multinational factories. While this is true, these workers, many of them women and children, often work 14 hours a day and earn less than €100 a month. One study of 15 countries found that **textile** workers earned less than 40% of the money they needed to live on each month. In some countries, this figure is even lower. Also, most workers are paid by the piece. This means they might earn only a few cents for making a dress which sells for hundreds of euros in Europe. Such low wages are wrong and unfair. As Priya Kapoor, a human rights researcher in Delhi, says, 'Garment workers in countries like India and Bangladesh can't afford to pay their basic needs like food and healthcare. We need to establish a fair wage for the work they do.'

3 Supporters of outsourcing also claim that overseas factories have become safer and more ethical in recent years. Some factories in China now provide day-care centres for their workers, for instance. But working **conditions** in many offshore factories remain uncomfortable and unsafe. Worker protection laws, like those in developed nations, often don't exist or are not followed. As a result, workers are exposed to chemicals, dust and unsafe levels of noise from sewing machines. I saw this myself when I visited a clothing factory in Bangladesh in 2017. The noise was so loud that I had to cover my ears. Moreover, factory buildings are often unsafe, and horrible accidents happen. For example, the whole world was shocked in 2012 when a fire broke out at a garment factory in Dhaka, Bangladesh, killing 117 people and injuring 200.

4 In conclusion, although supporters of outsourcing provide a number of convincing arguments, in my opinion these do not justify the low wages and dangerous conditions found in many overseas factories. If multinationals are going to continue to benefit from low production costs by using overseas suppliers, I believe they should contribute a much larger share of their massive profits to correcting these problems and improving social conditions in the countries where they are located.

WHILE READING

3 Skim the title and the first paragraph of the essay.

1 What is the essay about?

2 What do supporters of the essay topic say about it? What is the writer's point of view? How do you know?

SKIMMING

READING FOR MAIN IDEAS

4 Read the article and complete the table with arguments and counter-arguments from the reading. The first one has been done for you as an example.

> ~~Provides jobs at higher wages than local workers can make in agriculture.~~
> Most workers are paid by the piece.
> People in developing countries often line up to take jobs in multinational factories.
> Working conditions in many offshore factories remain uncomfortable and unsafe.
> Overseas factories have become safer and more ethical in recent years.
> Workers often work 14 hours a day and earn less than €100 a month.
> Worker protection laws, like those in developed nations, often don't exist or are not followed.

arguments for outsourcing	arguments against outsourcing
Provides jobs at higher wages than local workers can make in agriculture.	

SCANNING TO FIND INFORMATION

5 Complete the sentences with words from the article.

1 In 2015, the European Union imported approximately €_____ worth of clothing.

2 _____ companies outsource their production to countries where workers are paid less than they are in developed countries.

3 One study found that workers in offshore factories earned only _____ percent of the money they needed each month, even though they worked 14 hours a day.

4 In developing countries, worker protection laws often _____.

5 _____ people died in the Dhaka fire in 2012.

6 David Schneider is an _____.

READING BETWEEN THE LINES

> **SKILLS**
>
> ### Distinguishing fact from opinion
>
> When you read a text, you need to be able to decide which points are facts and which points are opinions. A *fact* is a true statement which, you can prove by looking at something or by doing research. An *opinion* usually expresses a person's idea, judgement or position. In fact, speakers and writers often use facts and reasons to support their opinions and make them sound convincing.

6 Look at the sentences from Reading 2 below and tick whether they are facts or the writer's opinion.

DISTINGUISHING FACT FROM OPINION

		fact	writer's opinion
1	… the European Union imported almost €29 billion worth of clothing in 2015.		
2	Supporters of outsourcing claim that it helps local economies, but I believe it is harmful for two main reasons.		
3	… most workers are paid by the piece. This means they might earn only a few cents for making a dress which sells for hundreds of euros in Europe.		
4	… worker-protection laws like those in developed nations often don't exist or are not followed.		
5	… working conditions in many offshore factories remain uncomfortable and unsafe.		
6	… although supporters of outsourcing provide a number of convincing arguments, in my opinion these do not justify the low wages and dangerous conditions found in many overseas factories.		

DISCUSSION

7 Work with a partner. Use ideas from Reading 1 and Reading 2 to answer the following questions.

1 These days the production of both designer fashion and fast fashion is outsourced to factories in developing countries. Do you think workers make more money if they are producing designer fashions? Do you think there is any difference in working conditions, depending on the type of fashion local workers are making?

2 Should multinationals that outsource to developing countries do more for the local community? What could they do?

SYNTHESIZING

LANGUAGE DEVELOPMENT

VOCABULARY FOR THE FASHION BUSINESS

1 Read the sentences (1–8) and write the correct form of the words in bold next to the definitions (a–h).

1 One of the biggest costs for retailers is **advertising**, but without it, customers have no way of getting information about shops and products.
2 Smart **consumers** shop for clothes during the off-season. For example, they buy winter coats in the spring.
3 Some shoppers only buy clothes made by **designer labels**. If it's not Gucci® or Prada®, they are not interested.
4 Forever 21® and H&M® are **competitors**. They have similar prices and they try to attract similar customers.
5 In the clothing business, most **manufacturing** is done in factories located in Asia or Latin America.
6 China and India are the two biggest **suppliers** of cotton in the world. Every big clothing company buys from them.
7 In some countries, workers are paid only 14 cents an hour for their **labour**.
8 As well as clothing companies, computer companies also find it cheaper to make their products **overseas**, mainly in Asia.

a _____ (n) a person or company that sells a product or service
b _____ (n) a company which makes or designs expensive clothes
c _____ (adv) in, from or to another country
d _____ (n) a person who buys a product or service for their own use
e _____ (n) the business of creating or sending out announcements in magazines, on television, etc. to attract shoppers
f _____ (n) a business which tries to win or do better than other businesses selling almost the same products
g _____ (n) work
h _____ (n) the process of making things, especially in a factory

WRITING

CRITICAL THINKING

At the end of this unit, you will write an argumentative essay. Look at this unit's writing task in the box below.

> The fashion industry is harmful to society and the environment.
> Do you agree or disagree?

Identifying strong arguments

Writers use *arguments* to support their opinions, and they also use *evidence* (facts, reasons, etc.) to support their arguments. Well-supported arguments persuade readers that the writer's opinion is true, correct or believable.

Common types of evidence in academic writing include facts, statistics, reasons, examples and personal experience. In addition, statements by experts are an especially strong type of evidence in academic texts.

1 Look at Reading 2 on page 155 and complete the table in note form. Then, write the author's conclusion.

UNDERSTAND

main argument: *Outsourcing is helpful.*	**supporting argument 1:** *Outsourcing provides jobs at higher wages.* **evidence:** 1 opinion of economist David Schneider 2 people line up for jobs
	author's response: *Outsourcing hurts workers.* **evidence:** 3 workers (men, women, children) often work 14 hours a day 4 _____ 5 _____ earn <40% of money needed 6 _____ 7 Priya Kapoor: people need a fair wage for their work.
	supporting argument 2: _____ **evidence:** 8 Factories in China _____
	author's response: *Working conditions are uncomfortable & dangerous.* **evidence:** 9 _____ 10 _____ 11 _____ author saw this first-hand 12 Fire in Dhaka, Bangladesh
	author's conclusion:

2 Work with a partner. Match each piece of evidence from the table in Exercise 1 to the relevant type of evidence. Write the numbers (1–12) in the table below.

facts	statistics	expert opinions	quotations	examples	personal experience

3 Work with a partner. Look at the types of evidence in the table above. Answer the questions.

1 Which type of evidence was used the most in Reading 2? Why do you think this type was used more than the others?
2 In your experience, which types of evidence are most common in academic writing?
3 Which types of evidence do you find most convincing? Why?

EVALUATE

4 Work with a partner. Read the Writing task on page 159 again. Decide if the arguments below are for or against the statement. Write F (for) or A (against).

1 creates new jobs ____
2 causes too much waste ____
3 encourages child labour ____
4 pays overseas workers badly ____
5 lets people show their personality ____
6 is important to the economy ____
7 allows people to change their look ____
8 pressures children to look like adults ____
9 makes children worry about their appearance ____
10 brings investment to developing countries ____

5 Look at the list of arguments in Exercise 4. Which arguments are stronger, those *for* or those *against* the statement? Why?

APPLY

6 Work with a partner. Choose the three strongest arguments *for* or *against* from Exercise 4. Write them in the table below. Then, for each argument, think of some supporting evidence or do research online. Try to use facts, statistics, reasons, examples, personal experience or quotations as evidence.

	argument	supporting evidence
1		
2		
3		

GRAMMAR FOR WRITING

MULTI-WORD PREPOSITIONS

> Some prepositions contain more than one word. These *multi-word prepositions* can be used to combine two pieces of information. In the following example, the two points are connected by the multi-word preposition *rather than*.
>
> *Critics of outsourcing claim that children should be in full-time education **rather than** working in a factory.*
>
> Common multi-word prepositions and their meanings include:
>
> **Reason:** *because of, due to, as a result of*   **Preference:** *rather than, instead of*
> **Exception:** *except for, other than, apart from*   **Contrast:** *in spite of*
> **Addition:** *in addition to, along with*   **Choice:** *instead of*

1 Read the sentences and underline the multi-word prepositions. What is the purpose of each preposition – *reason, exception, addition, preference, contrast* or *choice*?

1 The low cost of most fast fashion enables shoppers to buy several new sets of clothes each season instead of wearing the same outfits year after year. _____
2 Due to their longer lifespan, expensive designer clothes are more environmentally friendly than cheap clothes. _____
3 Because of the low labour costs in developing nations, multinational companies are able to keep most of the profits from the sale of the clothes produced overseas. _____
4 Conditions in some overseas factories are terrible. In spite of this, many local workers want to get jobs in these factories. _____
5 The United States, along with Europe and Japan, is the leading consumer of fast fashion. _____

2 Complete the sentences with multi-word prepositions from the Grammar box above.

1 The company closed its offshore production facilities _____ its overseas retail stores.
2 Most people prefer wearing casual clothes _____ formal business suits.
3 _____ perfume, I don't use any designer products.
4 _____ cheap overseas labour, people in developed countries can buy shirts for five euros.
5 Recently, I started buying some high-end clothes that last _____ fast fashion.

3 Complete the sentences with prepositions from the box.

> along with   except for   in addition to   in spite of   instead of

1 _____ buying fast fashion, it is better for the environment if people choose clothes which last longer.
2 _____ encouraging child labour, offshore production also drives wages and working conditions down.
3 _____ the low wages in overseas factories, many people are eager to take these jobs.
4 Workers can't wear any jewellery in the factory _____ wedding rings.
5 China, _____ the USA and India, is a world-leading exporter of cotton.

ACADEMIC WRITING SKILLS

BODY PARAGRAPHS IN POINT–COUNTERPOINT ESSAYS

SKILLS

The introductory paragraph of a point–counterpoint essay describes the issue and includes a thesis statement giving the writer's position. The introduction is followed by one or more body paragraphs in which the writer presents arguments that support his or her thesis. The goal of these paragraphs is to convince the reader to agree with the writer's point of view.

Each body paragraph has a topic sentence which presents the writer's supporting argument and the evidence to support that argument.

1 Read the thesis statement for an essay about the negative effects of the fashion industry on young people's body image (how they feel about their bodies). Read the possible topic sentences (a–d) from the paragraph below, and choose the one that best supports the thesis statement.

> Thesis statement: *The fashion industry has a negative influence on young people's body image and can cause serious issues, such as depression and eating problems.*

a Advertising companies use computer software to make photos of models look unrealistically perfect.
b The fashion industry's unrealistic image of the human body can cause young people to become depressed about how they look.
c Pressure from parents to do well in school or get a job can also cause young people to become depressed.
d Rates of depression are especially high among young adults between the ages of 18 and 30.

2 Read the body paragraph of a student's essay below. Then, circle the topic sentence, where the writer states his or her argument.

> Within the fashion industry, some magazines and designers have recently begun promoting a more positive and realistic body image in their products. A leading fashion magazine announced that it would encourage a healthier approach to body image in all its editions. Some fashion companies have begun to use models that have more realistic body types. In addition, Pierre Dupont, a French fashion designer, announced a new collection aimed at celebrating body diversity. 'I believe we should represent all body shapes,' he said.

3 What evidence does the writer use to support his or her argument in the body paragraph?

_____
_____

4 Work with a partner. Do you think the writer's argument and evidence are convincing? Why / Why not?

_____

COUNTER-ARGUMENTS

LANGUAGE

Look at the tables and examples below. They show some of the different ways to express the opinions of other people. Use these structures to include opinions that may be different from your own.

Supporters		are in favour of	
Critics	(of X)		Y.
Opponents		are against	

They	argue claim insist state point out	that X	is an important factor in plays a central role in plays an important part in has a positive/negative impact on leads to	Y (because ...).

Supporters of moving production overseas **are in favour of** foreign investment. **They insist that** this investment **plays a central role in** improving the economy in developing countries.

Critics of offshore production **are against** moving jobs abroad. **They claim that** this activity **leads to** unemployment in developed countries.

ACADEMIC WRITING SKILLS 163

5 Complete the sentences with words and phrases from the Language box on page 163. Sometimes more than one answer is possible.

1 Supporters of fast fashion are _____ of offshore production. They _____ that overseas manufacturing _____ the economy of developing countries.
2 _____ of fast fashion _____ that it is bad for the environment because it encourages people to throw clothes away.
3 Supporters of fast fashion are in favour of fashion advertising. They _____ that advertising _____ in helping the economy _____ it encourages people to spend more on clothes.

6 Look at Exercise 4 on page 160 and use the arguments to help you complete the sentences below.

1 Supporters of the fashion industry argue that _____ .
2 They claim that _____ .
3 They also state that _____ .
4 On the other hand, critics of the fashion industry point out that _____ and _____ .
5 They insist that _____ .

COHESION

> Cohesion refers to the way writers connect ideas in and between sentences. When writing is cohesive, it is clear and easy to follow. Writers use the following techniques to make writing cohesive:
>
> a transitions (changes) between sentences or between ideas
> b repetition of nouns or use of synonyms
> c pronouns that refer back to nouns in earlier sentences
> d *this/that/these/those* to refer to earlier nouns or ideas

7 Read the extracts from Reading 1. Then, underline and identify the cohesive techniques from the Skills box that are being used. The first one is done for you.

1 The fashion industry has changed significantly in recent years. <u>Traditionally</u>, fashion retailers created two clothing collections per year, called seasons. Nowadays, in contrast, they can design and manufacture clothes in as little as four weeks.
2 The low cost of most fast fashion enables shoppers to buy several new sets of clothes each season instead of wearing the same outfits year after year. This means that a huge amount of clothing is thrown away. Furthermore, with fashions changing so quickly, cotton growers need to produce more cotton more cheaply, and that means using more pesticides and chemicals.

8 Read the summary of some of the ideas in Readings 1 and 2. Complete the paragraph using the words in the box to make it cohesive.

> change   In addition   Meanwhile   ones
> that   them   these   they   this   This

The speed of change in the fashion world means that we buy many more clothes than we need. To keep up with (1)_____ fast pace of (2)_____ , retailers create a constant demand for new clothes by selling (3)_____ cheaply and changing items every week. To make space for the new clothes, customers throw away the old (4)_____ as soon as (5)_____ are out of style. (6)_____ way of shopping leads to a higher demand for cotton, and (7)_____ means more intensive agriculture and damage to the environment. (8)_____ , many of (9)_____ cheap clothes are sewn in sweatshops in countries where workers earn less than a euro a day. (10)_____ , the clothing companies keep nearly all the profits.

WRITING TASK

▌The fashion industry is harmful to society and the environment. Do you agree or disagree?

PLAN

1 Look at your list of arguments and supporting evidence in Exercise 6 in the Critical thinking section.

2 Use the outline below to plan your essay.

introductory paragraph	• Introduce the topic. • In the thesis statement, state your position. Mention the main counter-arguments.
body paragraphs (2–3)	• Give argument 1 and counter-argument 1 with supporting evidence. • Give argument 2 and counter-argument 2 with supporting evidence. • (Optional) Give argument 3 and counter-argument 3 with supporting evidence.
concluding paragraph	• Summarize the main arguments for and against. • Restate your position and any arguments and evidence that are particularly strong. • Make a strong final statement to convince your reader to agree with you.

WRITE A FIRST DRAFT

3 Answer the question in the Writing task by writing an essay with four paragraphs, following your plan in Exercise 2. Write 250–300 words.

REVISE

4 Use the Task checklist to review your essay for content and structure.

TASK CHECKLIST	✔
Does the introduction include a statement of your position and a sentence about the main counter-arguments?	
In the body paragraphs, did you present arguments and counter-arguments?	
Did you include evidence to support each argument?	
In the conclusion, did you repeat your position and summarize your arguments?	
Did you include a strong final statement to persuade the reader to agree with you?	

5 Make any necessary changes to your essay.

EDIT

6 Use the Language checklist to edit your essay for language errors.

LANGUAGE CHECKLIST	✔
Did you use vocabulary for the fashion business?	
Did you use multi-word prepositions correctly?	
Did you use cohesive devices to connect your ideas in and between sentences?	

7 Make any necessary changes to your essay.

OBJECTIVES REVIEW

1 Check your learning objectives for this unit. Write *3, 2* or *1* for each objective.

3 = very well   2 = well   1 = not so well

I can ...

watch and understand a video about Savile Row's first female Master Tailor.	_____
distinguish fact from opinion.	_____
identify strong arguments.	_____
use multi-word prepositions to combine information.	_____
use body paragraphs in point–counterpoint essays.	_____
use counter-arguments.	_____
use cohesion.	_____
write a point–counterpoint essay.	_____

2 Use the *Unlock* Digital Workbook for more practice with this unit's learning objectives.

WORDLIST

advertising (n)	import (v)	overseas (adv)
brand (n)	invest (v)	season (n)
collection (n)	labour (n)	supplier (n)
competitor (n)	manufacture (v)	textile (n)
conditions (n pl)	manufacturing (n)	volume (n)
consumer (n)	multinational (adj)	wage (n)
cotton (n)	offshore (adj)	
designer label (n)	outsource (v)	

= high-frequency words in the Cambridge Academic Corpus

LEARNING OBJECTIVES	IN THIS UNIT YOU WILL …
Watch and listen	watch and understand a video about the stock market crash of 1929.
Reading skill	skim for general ideas.
Critical thinking	understand and interpret line graphs.
Grammar	describe graphs using noun and verb phrases; use prepositions and conjunctions to add data; use approximations.
Academic writing skills	write a description of a graph; write a concluding paragraph.
Writing task	write an analysis essay.

ECONOMICS UNIT 8

UNLOCK YOUR KNOWLEDGE

Work with a partner. Discuss the questions.

1 Do you believe it is important for people to be informed about economics? Why / Why not?
2 What causes some countries to be rich and other countries to be poor? Why do you think there is such a big gap between the rich and the poor in some countries?
3 How has the economy of your country changed in recent years?

WATCH AND LISTEN

PREPARING TO WATCH

ACTIVATING YOUR KNOWLEDGE

1 Work with a partner. Discuss the questions.

1 What cities in the world today are centres of money and banking?
2 What happens during an economic depression?
3 How healthy is the economy of your country?

PREDICTING CONTENT

2 You are going to watch a video about a very bad day for the world economy. Before you watch, work with a partner and use the photos from the video and your own knowledge to answer the questions.

1 What do you think happened?
2 Where did it happen?
3 Did it happen recently or a long time ago?

> **GLOSSARY**
>
> **stock market** (n) a system for buying and selling parts of companies; the total value of all the investments that are traded in this system
>
> **crash** (v) to fall or lose value suddenly and completely
>
> **investor** (n) someone who puts money in a bank, business, etc. in order to make a profit
>
> **depression** (n) a period in which there is very little business activity and little employment
>
> **replica** (n) a copy of an object
>
> **ticker tape** (n) a long, thin strip of paper, used in the past for printing changing information on, for example, the prices of stocks

WHILE WATCHING

3 ▶ Watch the video. Check your answers to Exercise 2.

UNDERSTANDING MAIN IDEAS

4 ▶ Watch again. Match the sentence halves.
   1 The stock market _____
   2 On Black Tuesday, investors _____
   3 Millions of people _____
   4 The Great Depression _____
   5 Ticker tape machines _____

   a was the worst economic period in modern history.
   b were used to print the prices of stocks and shares.
   c crashed in 1929.
   d lost their jobs.
   e lost billions of dollars.

UNDERSTANDING DETAIL

5 ▶ Watch again. Answer the questions.
   1 When exactly did Black Tuesday happen? _____
   2 What happened to stock prices after Black Tuesday?
   _____
   3 What happened to many banks and companies? _____
   4 Where is the Museum of Financial History? _____
   5 What does the stock exchange use now to report stock prices?
   _____

MAKING INFERENCES

6 Work with a partner. Discuss the questions and give reasons for your answers.
   1 Were most financial experts surprised by Black Tuesday?
   2 Why did people in other countries lose their jobs during the Depression?
   3 How have computers changed stock markets?

DISCUSSION

7 Work in small groups. Discuss the questions.
   1 What are the biggest economic problems in the world today?
   2 How do changes in the economy affect your daily life?
   3 Do you think the economy will be better or worse in ten years? Why?

READING

READING 1

PREPARING TO READ

UNDERSTANDING KEY VOCABULARY

1 You are going to read an article about investments. Before you read the article, read the sentences (1–7) and write the words in bold next to the definitions (a–g).

1 During the **recession** of 2007–2009, people all over the world lost their jobs and were forced to sell their homes.
2 At my bank, the **interest rate** on a loan to buy a car is about 4.5%.
3 Since Apple Computer company **stocks and shares** went on sale in 1976, their value has increased by more than 28,000%.
4 Real estate, that is land or buildings, is an excellent **investment** in large cities like Los Angeles or Tokyo.
5 My father is a careful **investor**. He buys assets, like buildings and cars, that increase slowly over time.
6 After a natural disaster, such as a tsunami or fire, the homes and businesses in an area usually go down in **value**.
7 If you buy gold, you can probably expect to get a high rate of **return** on your investment.

a _____ (n) the percentage amount that you pay when you borrow money, or receive when you lend money, for a period of time
b _____ (n) profit on money you have invested
c _____ (n) parts of a publicly-owned business which can be bought and sold as investments
d _____ (n) someone who puts money in a bank, business, etc. to make a profit
e _____ (n) how much money something could be sold for
f _____ (n) a period when the economy of a country is not doing well, but not as bad as a depression
g _____ (n) something such as stocks or property which you buy in order to make a profit

USING YOUR KNOWLEDGE

2 Work with a partner. Discuss the questions.
1 Can you think of some usual and unusual ways to invest money? What are they?
2 Can you give an example of a safe investment? What investments are risky?
3 Two possible investments are gold and classic cars. Do you think they are safe, risky or somewhere in-between? Which do you think has been more profitable recently?

How should you invest your money?

1 In a **recession**, **interest rates** are low. This means that keeping your money in a bank may not be the best way of making money. **Stocks and shares** are also risky when the economy takes a dive[1]. So where should you invest to make the most of your money? For the brave **investor**, there is a range of alternative **investments**. Gold and classic cars are two popular investments because their market **value** tends to go up with time.

2 Over time, gold has been a very good investment, though the price has fluctuated[2] in recent years, as the graph below shows. Between 2009 and 2012, for example, the price rose from $1,087 an ounce to a peak of $1,664 an ounce. Then, by the end of 2015, it had fallen to $1,161. In 2016, it rose slightly again to $1,249. Forecasters expect it to stay in this range until 2025. If you are thinking about investing in gold, you may want to consider one famous investor's advice. Warren Buffet, one of the richest men in the world, dislikes gold as an investment. He points out that historically, the stock market has brought in significantly higher **returns** than gold. He also says it is better for society if you use your money for something productive, rather than have it sitting in a bank.

3 While gold and stocks are both excellent investment options in the long term, some people prefer investments that they can use and enjoy. For these people, classic cars are one way to have fun and make lots of money. In fact, over the last 30 or 40 years, the value of some classic cars has risen far more than that of gold or other investments like houses. As an example, a 1972 Ferrari Dino 246 GT cost around $13,000 in 1980 but was worth as much as $450,000 in 2016. A 1955 Mercedes-Benz 300SL cost about $36,000 in 1980 but is worth about $1 million now. But neither of these cars compares to what is perhaps the best investment ever: a man in Tennessee bought the Aston Martin DB5 which was used in two of the James Bond films. This car cost just $7,000 in 1980 but sold in 2010 for an incredible $4.1 million! That is an incredible 20,000% increase!

4 In sum, the prospect of making lots of money through investing is very exciting, but one must never forget that investing is a risky business. Gold prices rise, but they also fall. Classic cars need to be kept in excellent condition to increase in value and, because fashions change, investors have to guess which car to invest in. If you are clever and lucky, you may make a big profit – but remember, there are no guarantees.

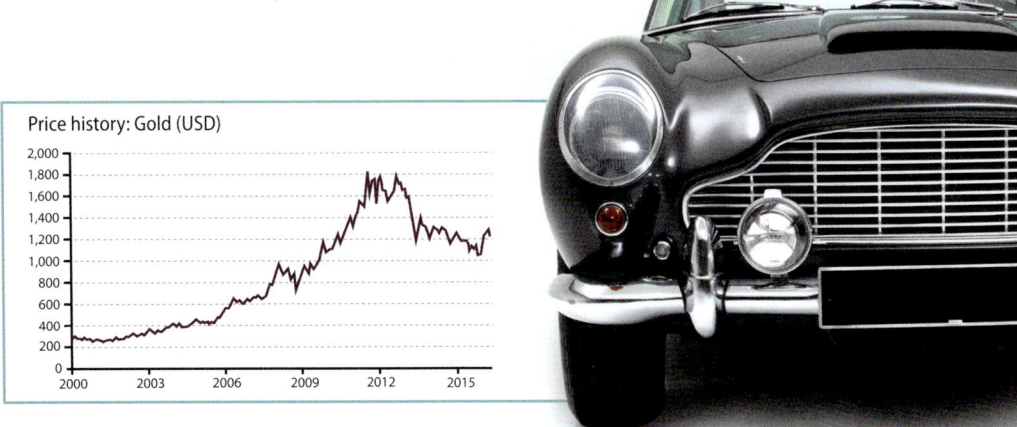

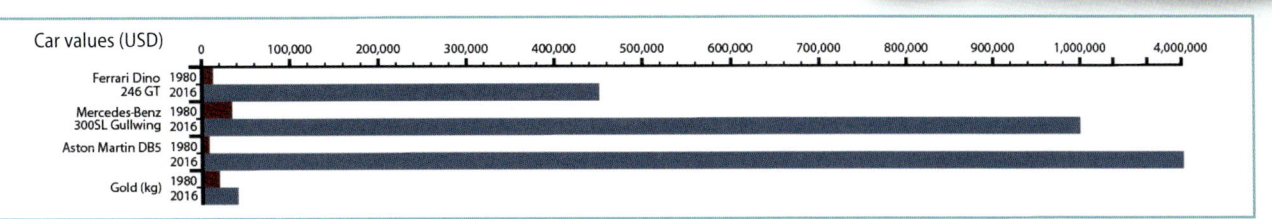

[1] **take a dive** (v) If a value or price takes a dive, it suddenly becomes less.

[2] **fluctuate** (v) to keep changing, especially in level or amount

WHILE READING

Skimming for general ideas

Skimming is the opposite of reading in depth. To skim a text, read it quickly to get a general idea of what it is about. Don't read every word. It is enough to read the title, the introductory paragraph, the concluding paragraph and perhaps the first sentence of each main body paragraph. It is also useful to look at any photos or diagrams in the text. Skimming is a particularly useful skill in academic reading.

SKIMMING

3 Skim the article and the graphs on page 173. Tick the topics that the article discusses.

- [ ] causes of a recession
- [ ] two popular investments
- [ ] the price of gold over time
- [ ] the stock market in 2016
- [ ] classic cars as an investment
- [ ] the risks of investing

READING FOR MAIN IDEAS

4 Look at your answers to Exercise 3. Find the main ideas and write them in the order that they appear in the reading.

Paragraph 1 _____
Paragraph 2 _____
Paragraph 3 _____
Paragraph 4 _____

READING FOR DETAIL

5 Read the article. Answer the questions using information from the article. Remember that you can annotate the text as you read.

1 Approximately how much did gold cost per ounce in 2009? _____

2 In which year was the price of gold the highest? How much did it cost per ounce? _____

3 According to forecasters, what will happen to the price of gold between now and 2025? _____

4 How much did a Ferrari Dino 246 GT cost in 1980? _____

5 What is a 1955 Mercedes-Benz 300SL worth now? _____

6 How much did the Aston Martin used in the James Bond films sell for in 2010? _____

READING BETWEEN THE LINES

MAKING INFERENCES

6 Work with a partner. Discuss the questions.

1 If you followed Warren Buffett's advice, would you invest in the stock market or in gold? Why?

2 Are classic cars a risky investment? Why / Why not?

3 As far as you know, what is the safest investment in general? Which investments do you think are the safest during a recession?

DISCUSSION

7 Work with a partner. Discuss the questions.

1 Imagine that you and your partner have one million pounds to invest. How would you invest the money? Why?
2 Are there any investments that you definitely would not make? Why would you choose not to invest your money in this way?
3 If you could afford it, would you buy an Aston Martin DB5? Why / Why not?

READING 2

PREPARING TO READ

UNDERSTANDING KEY VOCABULARY

1 You are going to read an article about income and expenditure. Before you read the article, read the sentences (1–6) below and write the words in bold next to the definitions (a–f).

1 My family has a comfortable **standard of living**. We have enough money to pay for everything we need, and we are able to save a little bit of money every month.
2 People who go to university usually have a higher **income** than people with only a secondary-school education.
3 Housing is the biggest **expenditure** for most people. For instance, many Europeans pay 40% or more of their income in rent or house payments.
4 The weather is one **factor** which influences the price of food. For example, if there is not enough rain, crops are smaller and the price of food goes up.
5 Families with many children must spend a large **percentage** of their income on food and clothing.
6 It is a good idea for workers to put some money into **savings** every month. Even putting a little aside each month can result in a large amount over time.

a _____ (n pl) money that you put away, usually in a bank, for a later date
b _____ (n) how much money and comfort someone has
c _____ (n) one of the things that has an effect on a particular situation, decision, event, etc.
d _____ (n) the total amount of money that a government or person spends on something
e _____ (n) money that you earn by working, investing or producing goods
f _____ (n) an amount of something, expressed as a number out of 100

USING YOUR KNOWLEDGE

2 Work with a partner. Answer the questions.
  1 Do you think the standard of living in most developed countries has improved, got worse or stayed the same in the last 20 years? _____
  2 What factor or factors play an important role in people's standard of living? _____

3 Scan the article and check your answers.

WHILE READING

ANNOTATING

4 Read and annotate the article opposite. Look at page 85 for what to annotate.

READING FOR MAIN IDEAS

5 Choose the sentence which best summarizes the article.
  a The article compares income and expenditure in the United States with the same factors in other developed countries.
  b The article explains how falling incomes and rising expenditure has affected people's standard of living in recent years.
  c The article describes five categories of expenditure which play a key role in determining people's standard of living.
  d The article discusses how the so-called 'economic miracle' became a reality for Japanese people in the years during and following the Second World War.

READING FOR DETAIL

6 Read the article again and choose the correct statement from each pair.
  1 a Incomes in the United States rose quickly in the 1970s, and have been increasing slowly since then.
    b Incomes in the United States fell from the 1980s to the 2000s and have been increasing slowly since then.
  2 a Between 1999 and 2016, median income in the US stayed about the same.
    b Between 1999 and 2016, median income fell by about 7%.
  3 a Between 2000 and 2016, Americans spent more on transport than they did on food.
    b Between 2000 and 2016, Americans' biggest expenditure was housing.
  4 a Healthcare costs have stayed approximately the same in spite of rising hospital costs.
    b Because of higher prices for prescription drugs and hospital stays, healthcare costs have increased.
  5 a Over the past two decades, people in developed countries have had less money to spend on entertainment and small luxuries like eating in restaurants.
    b Over the past two decades, people in developed countries have been able to spend more money on entertainment and small luxuries like eating in restaurants.

FALLING INCOME, RISING EXPENDITURE

1 In almost every country and every culture, parents work hard to try to give their children a richer, more successful and more comfortable life than they had. For decades following the Second World War, this dream became a reality in many countries around the world. Possibly the best example is the Japanese 'economic miracle', when Japan, thanks to an extremely high rate of economic growth from the 1960s to the 1980s, developed into one of the world's strongest economies. Yet in Japan, as in other developed nations, many people today are not able to enjoy the same **standard of living** as their parents before them. This is because in recent years, **incomes** have declined while **expenditure** has risen. In effect, this means many people are actually poorer than they were 10 or 20 years ago.

2 Falling incomes are the first cause of a declining standard of living. In the United States, for instance, incomes rose during the 1970s, began falling in the 1980s, and reached their low point during the Great Recession of 2007–2009. The years since then have seen a slow recovery; yet according to the US Census Bureau, the median[1] income in 2016 was $59,039 – nearly the same as in 1999. Similarly, in the United Kingdom, the average household income of £25,700 in 2016 was nearly the same as that in 2007.

3 The other key **factor** which influences people's standard of living is expenditure. Worldwide, prices for necessities such as rent and food have been rising. As an example, Figure 1 shows the **percentage** of their income that Americans spent on five key categories between 2000 and 2016: housing, food, transport, entertainment and health. Until 2015, the costs in these five categories remained more or less stable. That is, Americans spent approximately 20% of their incomes on housing, about 10% on food, about 8% on transport, and around 3% each on entertainment and health. As the graph shows, most of these costs jumped in 2015 and have continued to rise.

4 In the United States and in many other countries, the most important cause of rising expenditure over time is the high cost of housing. In many cities worldwide there is a critical shortage of houses and apartments to buy and rent. This has driven up costs. Also, healthcare costs continue to rise as prescription drugs and hospital costs have become more and more expensive. Transport and food prices have also increased significantly in recent years.

5 In conclusion, the combination of rising prices and falling incomes has left many people with less spending power than they had in previous decades. Because consumers must pay more for essentials like food, healthcare and especially housing, they have less money for education, investment, **savings** and small luxuries like eating in restaurants. For many people, the dream of living in greater comfort and security than their parents must seem very distant indeed.

[1] **median** (adj) having a value that is exactly in the middle of a set of values arranged from largest to smallest

Figure 1

MAKING INFERENCES

READING BETWEEN THE LINES

7 Work with a partner. Answer the questions.

1 What are some examples of countries that became richer in the decades following the Second World War?
_____

2 What are some causes of the shortage of housing in cities worldwide?
_____

3 If the average American earned around $59,000 in 2016, about how much did that person spend on housing?
_____

SYNTHESIZING

DISCUSSION

8 Work with a partner. Use ideas from Reading 1 and Reading 2 to answer the following questions.

1 Do people in most developed countries probably have more, less or about the same amount of money to invest as they did before the Great Recession of 2007–2009? Why?
2 If someone's income is falling and expenditure is rising, is it a good idea to try to make more money by investing in the stock market, gold, etc.? Why / Why not?
3 What has happened to income and expenditure in your country since 1996? Why?

⊙ LANGUAGE DEVELOPMENT

NOUNS AND ADJECTIVES FOR ECONOMICS

1 Use a dictionary to find the meanings of the words in the table and write the definitions.

noun	adjective
1 economy	economic
2 finance	financial
3 wealth	wealthy
4 poverty	poor
5 value	valuable
6 employment	employed
7 profession	professional
8 expense	expensive

2 Complete the sentences using either an adjective or a noun from the table in Exercise 1 on the opposite page.

1 Since 2012, the US _____ has been weak, with little growth.
2 Companies that are losing money often turn to the banks for _____ assistance.
3 Only _____ investors can afford to buy expensive classic cars.
4 As incomes have fallen in recent years, more and more people have fallen into _____ .
5 Many wealthy people enjoy spending their money to buy _____ art.
6 Each year the OECD (Organization for Economic Cooperation and Development) publishes _____ statistics on how many people in its member countries are working.
7 _____ services like legal or financial advice can cost a lot of money.
8 It is _____ to buy even a single share in some successful companies, so you might want to start investing with companies whose shares are relatively inexpensive.

NOUNS FOR ECONOMIC TRENDS

3 Read the definitions and complete the sentences with the correct form of the words in bold.

> **consumer** (n) a person who buys a product or service to use
> **demand** (n) the need for something to be sold or supplied
> **market** (n) the total number of people who might want to buy something
> **purchase** (n) something that you buy
> **revenue** (n) the income that a company or government receives
> **supply** (n) an amount or quantity of something available to use
> **trend** (n) the general direction of changes or developments

1 The top world _____ for fast fashion are developed countries such as the United Kingdom, Italy and Japan.
2 I was not satisfied with my _____ , so I returned the item to the shop.
3 When shopping for large items like cars and refrigerators, clever _____ compare prices before they make their decision.
4 A recent fashion _____ for women is shoes with extremely high heels.
5 The company failed because there was not enough _____ for the products it was selling.
6 _____ from movie downloads has increased by more than 200% since 2010.
7 Prices go up when there is not enough _____ of a product or service that people want.

WRITING

CRITICAL THINKING

At the end of this unit, you will write an analysis essay about a graph. Look at this unit's writing task in the box below.

> Describe the multiple-line graph comparing revenue from DVD sales and video streaming and explain the data.

Understanding line graphs

A line graph uses points on a line to show a trend. Use the following strategies to read and understand a line graph:

- Read the title. It gives the subject of the graph and often summarizes the most important trend that the data shows.
- The time period covered by the graph appears on the horizontal axis of the graph, that is, the line that goes from left to right along the bottom. Is it in years, months, weeks or days?
- Now look at the vertical axis – the line that goes from top to bottom on the left side of the graph. This axis shows numbers or percentages.
- To 'read' a line graph, notice how the line in the centre of the graph shows a number or percentage on the vertical axis and a point of time on the horizontal axis.
- Many line graphs have more than one line. In this way, one graph can show more than one trend. Each line will have a different colour or pattern. Look for the *legend* – the box or sentence that explains what each colour or pattern means.

UNDERSTAND

1 Work with a partner. Look at the graph from Reading 2 on page 177. Answer the questions to help you read and understand the graph.

　1 What trend or 'main idea' does the graph show? _____

　2 What is the meaning of the numbers on the left side of the graph? _____

　3 Which years are covered by the graph? _____

　4 Why does the graph have five lines in different colours? What does each colour mean? _____

　5 What percentage of their income did Americans spend on food in 2016? _____

　6 From 2000 to 2006, did the percentage of income that Americans spent on transport increase or decrease? _____

　7 What trend do you see starting in 2006? Is it the same for all five types of expenditure? _____

> ### Interpreting a line graph
> Once you have understood the information in a line graph, you need to interpret it. This means identifying relationships between the points on the graph and trying to explain any trends that you notice in the data. (Note: graphs contain facts, not reasons. You will need to use your own information or do research in order to interpret the data.) If the graph has more than one line, you also need to identify the relationships between the sets of data.

2 Work with a partner. Look at the graph on page 177 again and answer the questions.

1 The graph shows one trend between 2000 and 2006 and another between 2006 and 2016. How do you explain these trends?

___

2 Between 2000 and 2016, which of the five types of expenditure went up and down most often? Why do you think this expenditure changed more than any of the others?

___

3 Which expenditure did not change between 2000 and 2014? Why?

___

4 What happened in 2015? Do you think this change was caused by a particular event, or is it normal for expenditure to change this way from time to time?

___

5 Based on the information in the graph, what can you conclude about Americans' standard of living in 2016?

___

3 Work with a partner. Look at the graph below. Answer the questions to help you read and understand the graph.

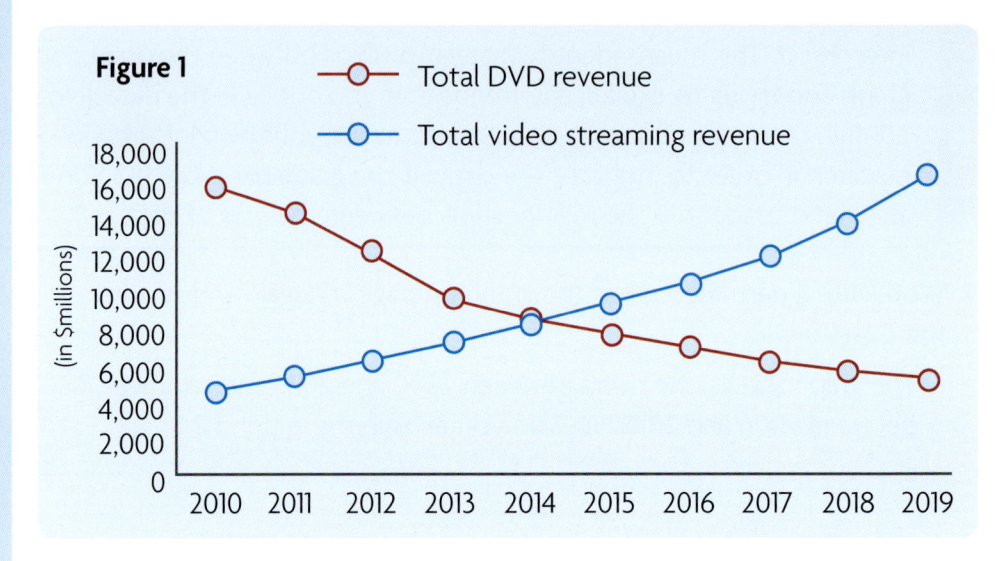

Figure 1
— Total DVD revenue
— Total video streaming revenue

(vertical axis: in $millions, 0 to 18,000; horizontal axis: years 2010–2019)

1 The graph compares DVD and video streaming revenue. What do these terms mean? Which line on the graph represents which term?
_____
_____

2 Which years are covered? _____
3 What is the meaning of the numbers on the vertical axis?
_____

4 In what year did revenue from sales of DVDs equal revenue from video streaming? _____

4 Complete the summary with figures from the graph.

In 2010, revenue from DVD sales was worth about $ (1)_____ m, compared to only about $ (2)_____ m for video streaming. Estimated revenues for these two types of media show the exact opposite picture in (3)_____ .

5 Answer the following questions to help you interpret the graph.

1 Summarize the trend shown in the graph. Complete this sentence: According to the graph, revenues from DVD sales and video streaming sales have moved in opposite directions. As revenue from sales of (1)_____ has risen, revenue from sales of (2)_____ has fallen.

2 What reason or reasons can you think of to explain the trend in Question 1?
_____
_____

3 Why is 2014 an important year in this graph?

GRAMMAR FOR WRITING

DESCRIBING GRAPHS USING NOUN AND VERB PHRASES

> You can describe data with a *verb phrase* (a verb + an adverb) or a *noun phrase* (an article + an adjective + a noun).
>
> Verb phrase
> Sales of DVDs **rose sharply** and then **decreased sharply**.
>
> Noun phrase
> There was **a sharp rise** in sales of DVDs and then **a sharp decrease**.
>
> You can use the verb *fluctuate* when the figures go up and down a lot.
> Our sales **fluctuated considerably** last year.

1 Match the sentences (1–6) to the graphs (a–f), which all refer to DVD sales.

1 Sales of DVDs rose sharply and then fell dramatically. _____
2 DVD sales decreased slightly and then decreased sharply. _____
3 The number of DVD sales did not change. _____
4 DVD sales increased slightly and then increased sharply. _____
5 At first, the number of DVDs sold did not change, but later this figure fluctuated. _____
6 DVD sales fell slightly but did not change after that. _____

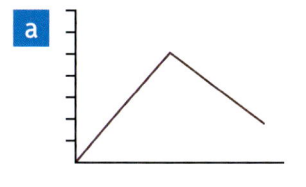

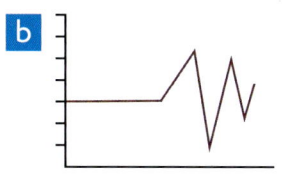

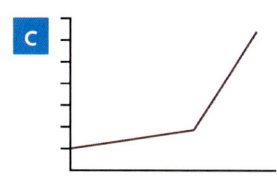

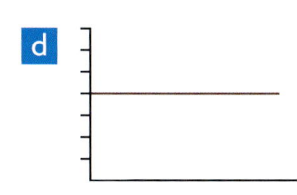

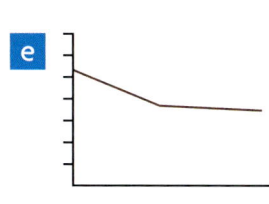

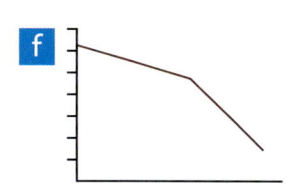

2 Write the verb phrases as noun phrases.

1 rise sharply   *a sharp rise*
2 fall dramatically   _____
3 decrease slightly   _____
4 increase gradually   _____
5 fluctuate considerably   _____

PREPOSITIONS AND CONJUNCTIONS

> You can use prepositions and conjunctions (*and, or, but,* etc.) to add data.
> Sales increased sharply **from** 7.68 **to** 10.63 million units **between** 2016 **and** 2018.
> You can use *of* in a noun phrase to describe the total change.
> This was an increase **of** 2.95 million units.

3 Complete the sentences using the words in bold in the examples above.

1 Sales fell _____ 1.1 million _____ 1 million units, a decrease _____ 100,000 units.
2 Prices rose _____ around £5.00 _____ well over £10.00 – a rise _____ 100%.
3 _____ 2008 _____ 2009, prices decreased slightly, _____ £7.75 _____ £7.00.
4 Prices fluctuated considerably _____ 2010 _____ 2018.
5 There was a gradual increase in prices _____ £8.00 _____ £8.95 during the last six months of the year.

USING APPROXIMATIONS

4 When we do not know exact figures, we can use words to show that the numbers we state are approximations (not exact). Fill in the blanks with words and phrases from the box that have the same meaning as the first word in each row.

> about   approximately   around   nearly   over   under

1 almost _____
2 more than _____
3 roughly _____ _____ _____
4 less than _____

5 Match the phrases to the figures.

1 almost a hundred euros   a €11,156
2 roughly a thousand euros   b €485,134
3 over ten thousand euros   c €240,000
4 more than eleven thousand euros d €1,014
5 less than a quarter of a million euros e €10,237
6 roughly half a million euros   f €996,001
7 approximately a million euros   g €99.99

ACADEMIC WRITING SKILLS

WRITING A DESCRIPTION OF A GRAPH

1 Read the description of a graph below. Then match the parts of the paragraph (1–3) to the labels (a–f). Not all of the labels are used.

> 1 The graph shows the sales figures for two types of mobile phone over an eight-year period.
> 2 In year 1, 40,000 units of phone A were sold. Sales of phones increased sharply for the next three years to reach a peak of 200,000, but decreased slightly in year 5. Sales dropped dramatically in years 6 and 7 to 30,000, as a result of the popularity of phone B. In year 8, only 5,000 units of phone A were sold. Sales of phone B grew gradually in years 1 and 2, from 60,000 to 65,000. Then, in years 3 to 6, there was a dramatic increase in the sales units for the phone as it became better known, peaking at 250,000. There was a slight decrease in year 7 and then the number of phones sold fell dramatically in year 8 to only 120,000 units.
> 3 The graph suggests that sales of phone B will probably drop further in the next year or so.

a Introductory sentence – explains what happened to sales in year one _____
b Introductory sentence – explains what can be seen on the graph _____
c Main part of the paragraph – highlights key points _____
d Main part of the paragraph – explains all the changes _____
e Concluding sentence – summarizes the changes, predicts what will happen in the future, or makes a final comment about the topic of the paragraph _____
f Concluding sentence – explains the last trends on the graph _____

2 Using the graph on page 182 to help you, draw the graph described in Exercise 1 above. Write the years 1–8 along the horizontal axis. Write the numbers 0–250 in bands of 50 up the vertical axis. In the centre of the graph draw two lines, according to the information about phone A and phone B.

3 Work with a partner. Compare your graphs. Discuss the following questions.
  1 What trends can be seen in the graph?
  2 How were sales of phone A and phone B similar over the period of the graph? How were they different?

WRITING A CONCLUDING PARAGRAPH

The concluding paragraph of an academic essay should end the essay without adding any new main ideas. It should be shorter than the body of the essay. Typically, this paragraph has three parts:

- **a transition phrase.** Transition phrases show that there is a link between the concluding paragraph and the previous paragraphs. Common phrases include: *In conclusion, In short, In summary, To summarize, To sum up* or *To conclude.*
- **a restatement or repetition of the thesis statement from the introduction.** Strategies for restating include changing the order of phrases and clauses, and using different words for the same concepts or ideas. For words that do not have synonyms, it is fine to repeat them in your conclusion.
- **a final comment.** This is your final message to your reader. It can be your opinion, a prediction about the future, a recommendation, a call to action on the part of the reader or a combination of these. If you are writing about a graph, it is common to conclude by stating the possible effects or consequences of the data.

4 Read the thesis statement and last paragraph of Reading 2 below. Then:
   1 underline the sentence in the concluding paragraph which restates the thesis.
   2 circle the transition phrase in the concluding paragraph.
   3 put a box around the final comments in the concluding paragraph. Which of the following does the writer include? Choose more than one.
      a an opinion
      b a prediction about the future
      c a recommendation
      d the implications of the data in the graph

Thesis statement
… in recent years, incomes have declined while expenditure has risen. In effect, this means many people are actually poorer than they were 10 or 20 years ago.

Concluding paragraph
In conclusion, the combination of rising prices and falling incomes has left many people with less spending power than they had in previous decades. Because consumers must pay more for essentials like food, healthcare and especially housing, they have less money for education, investment, savings and small luxuries like eating in restaurants. For many people, the dream of living in greater comfort and security than their parents must seem very distant indeed.

WRITING TASK

> Describe the multiple-line graph comparing revenue from DVD sales and video streaming and explain the data.

PLAN

1 Look at the questions you answered in Exercises 3–5 of the Critical thinking section.

2 Plan your introductory paragraph. Write notes for the hook, background information and thesis statement of your introduction.

3 Outline the body of your essay. It should have two paragraphs. You should describe the graph in the first paragraph. You should interpret the data in the second paragraph.

4 Plan your concluding paragraph. It should restate your thesis statement and include final remarks.

5 Use the Task checklist below as you prepare your essay.

WRITE A FIRST DRAFT

6 Write the first draft of your essay using your essay plan. Write 250–300 words.

REVISE

7 Use the Task checklist to review your essay for content and structure.

TASK CHECKLIST	✔
Does your introduction include a hook, background information and a thesis statement?	
Did you write two body paragraphs, one describing the graph and one interpreting the graph?	
Did you refer to the graph in the body paragraphs?	
Did you write a concluding paragraph that restates the thesis and includes final remarks?	

8 Make any necessary changes to your essay.

EDIT

9 Use the Language checklist to edit your essay for language errors.

LANGUAGE CHECKLIST	✔
Did you use nouns and adjectives for economics (e.g. *finance, financial*)?	
Did you use nouns for economic trends (e.g. *trend, consumer, market*)?	
Did you vary your language, using noun phrases, verb phrases and synonyms to describe graphs?	
Did you use prepositions and conjunctions (e.g. *from, to, between, and, of*) to add data?	
Did you use words and phrases for approximations (*more than, under, around, roughly,* etc.)?	

10 Make any necessary changes to your essay.

OBJECTIVES REVIEW

1 Check your learning objectives for this unit. Write *3, 2* or *1* for each objective.

3 = very well   2 = well   1 = not so well

I can ...

watch and understand a video about the stock market crash of 1929. _____

skim for general ideas. _____

understand and interpret line graphs. _____

describe graphs using noun and verb phrases. _____

use prepositions and conjunctions to add data. _____

use approximations. _____

write a description of a graph. _____

write a concluding paragraph. _____

write an analysis essay. _____

2 Use the *Unlock* Digital Workbook for more practice with this unit's learning objectives.

WORDLIST

consumer (n)	investment (n)	revenue (n)
demand (n)	investor (n)	savings (n pl)
economy (n)	market (n)	standard of living (n)
employment (n)	percentage (n)	stocks and shares (n)
expenditure (n)	poverty (n)	supply (n)
factor (n)	professional (adj)	trend (n)
financial (adj)	purchase (n)	valuable (adj)
income (n)	recession (n)	value (n)
interest rate (n)	return (n)	wealthy (adj)

◉ = high-frequency words in the Cambridge Academic Corpus

GLOSSARY

◉ = high-frequency words in the Cambridge Academic Corpus

Vocabulary	Pronunciation	Part of speech	Definition
UNIT 1			
affect ◉	/əˈfekt/	(v)	to influence or cause something to change
attach	/əˈtætʃ/	(v)	to connect or join one thing to another
chemical ◉	/ˈkemɪkəl/	(n)	a man-made or natural solid, liquid or gas made by changing atoms
common ◉	/ˈkɒmən/	(adj)	happening often or existing in large numbers
contrast ◉	/kənˈtrɑːst/	(v)	to show or explain differences between two people, situations or things
cooperate	/kəʊˈɒpəreɪt/	(v)	to work together for a particular purpose
cruel	/ˈkruːəl/	(adj)	causing pain or making someone or something suffer on purpose
destroy ◉	/dɪˈstrɔɪ/	(v)	to damage something very badly; to cause it to not exist
disease ◉	/dɪˈziːz/	(n)	illness; a serious health condition which requires care
due to	/djuː tə/	(prep)	because of; as a result of
endangered	/ɪnˈdeɪndʒəd/	(adj)	(of plants and animals) that may disappear soon
fatal ◉	/ˈfeɪtəl/	(adj)	causing death
introduce ◉	/ˌɪntrəˈdjuːs/	(v)	to put something into a place for the first time
major ◉	/ˈmeɪdʒə/	(adj)	most serious or important

Vocabulary	Pronunciation	Part of speech	Definition
native	/ˈneɪtɪv/	(adj)	used to describe animals and plants which grow naturally in a place
natural	/ˈnætʃərəl/	(adj)	as found in nature; not made or caused by people
pollute	/pəˈluːt/	(v)	to make the air, water or land dirty and unhealthy
protect	/prəˈtekt/	(v)	to keep something or someone safe from damage or injury
release	/rɪˈliːs/	(v)	to allow someone or something to leave a place
species	/ˈspiːʃiːz/	(n)	a group of plants or animals which are the same in some way
survive	/səˈvaɪv/	(v)	to stay alive; to continue to exist, especially after an injury or threat

UNIT 2

Vocabulary	Pronunciation	Part of speech	Definition
absorb	/əbˈzɔːb/	(v)	to take in a liquid or gas through a surface and hold it
annual	/ˈænjuəl/	(adj)	happening or produced once a year
area	/ˈeəriə/	(n)	regions of a country or city
atmosphere	/ˈætməsfɪə/	(n)	the layer of gases around the Earth
cause	/kɔːz/	(n)	someone or something that makes something happen
challenge	/ˈtʃælɪndʒ/	(n)	something that is difficult and that tests someone's ability or determination
climate	/ˈklaɪmət/	(n)	the general weather conditions usually found in a particular place
consequences	/ˈkɒnsɪkwənsɪz/	(n)	the results of an action or situation, especially bad results
construction	/kənˈstrʌkʃən/	(n)	the process of building something, usually large structures such as houses, roads or bridges

Vocabulary	Pronunciation	Part of speech	Definition
contribute to	/kənˈtrɪbjuːt tə/	(phr v)	to be one of the causes of an event or a situation
destruction	/dɪˈstrʌkʃən/	(n)	the act of causing so much damage to something that it stops existing because it cannot be repaired
ecosystem	/ˈiːkəʊsɪstəm/	(n)	all the living things in an area and the effect they have on each other and the environment
effect	/ɪˈfekt/	(n)	result; a change which happens because of a cause
farming	/ˈfɑːmɪŋ/	(n)	the job of working on a farm or organizing work on a farm
fossil fuel	/ˈfɒsəl ˌfjuːəl/	(n)	a source of energy like coal, gas and petroleum, that was formed inside the Earth millions of years ago
global warming	/ˌgləʊbəl ˈwɔːmɪŋ/	(n)	an increase in the Earth's temperature because of pollution
greenhouse gas	/ˌgriːnhaʊs ˈgæs/	(n)	a gas which makes the air around the Earth warmer
issue	/ˈɪʃuː/	(n)	an important subject or problem that people are discussing
logging	/ˈlɒgɪŋ/	(n)	the activity or business of cutting down trees for wood
predict	/prɪˈdɪkt/	(v)	to say what you think will happen in the future
rainforest	/ˈreɪnfɒrɪst/	(n)	a forest in a tropical area with a rainfall of 250 cm or more per year
threaten	/ˈθretən/	(v)	to be likely to damage or harm something
trend	/trend/	(n)	a general development or change in a situation

Vocabulary	Pronunciation	Part of speech	Definition
UNIT 3			
attempt ◉	/əˈtempt/	(v)	if you make an attempt to do something, you try to do it
commuter	/kəˈmjuːtə/	(n)	someone who travels between home and work, or university, regularly
connect ◉	/kəˈnekt/	(v)	to join two things or places together
consider ◉	/kənˈsɪdər/	(v)	to think carefully about a decision or something you might do
convince	/kənˈvɪns/	(v)	to make someone believe that something is true
cycle ◉	/ˈsaɪkəl/	(v)	to travel by bicycle
destination	/ˌdestɪˈneɪʃən/	(n)	the place where someone or something is going
emergency ◉	/ɪˈmɜːdʒənsi/	(n)	an unexpected situation which requires immediate action
engineering ◉	/ˌendʒɪˈnɪərɪŋ/	(n)	the activity of designing and building things like bridges, roads, machines, etc.
fuel ◉	/ˈfjuːəl/	(n)	a substance like gas or coal which produces energy when it is burnt
government ◉	/ˈgʌvənmənt/	(n)	the group of people that controls a country or city and makes decisions about laws, taxes, education, etc.
outskirts	/ˈaʊtskɜːts/	(n)	the outer area of a city or town
practical ◉	/ˈpræktɪkəl/	(adj)	useful; suitable for the situation it is being used for
prevent ◉	/prɪˈvent/	(v)	to stop something happening or to stop someone doing something
produce ◉	/prəˈdjuːs/	(v)	to make or grow something
public transport	/ˌpʌblɪk ˈtrænspɔːt/	(n)	a system of vehicles, such as buses and trains, which operate at regular times for public use

Vocabulary	Pronunciation	Part of speech	Definition
rail	/reɪl/	(n)	the form of transport which uses trains
reduce 👁	/rɪˈdjuːs/	(v)	to make something less
require 👁	/rɪˈkwaɪə/	(v)	to need or demand something
traffic congestion	/ˈtræfɪk kənˈdʒestʃən/	(n)	when too many vehicles use a road network and it results in slower speeds, or no movement at all
vehicle 👁	/ˈviːɪkəl/	(n)	any machine which travels on roads, such as cars, buses, etc.
waste 👁	/weɪst/	(v)	to use too much of something, or use something badly, when there is a limited amount of it

UNIT 4

Vocabulary	Pronunciation	Part of speech	Definition
appearance 👁	/əˈpɪərəns/	(n)	the way someone or something looks
belief 👁	/bɪˈliːf/	(n)	an idea that you are sure is true
brief 👁	/briːf/	(adj)	short
ceremony	/ˈserɪməni/	(n)	a formal event with special traditions, activities or words, such as a wedding
certain 👁	/ˈsɜːtən/	(adj)	used to refer to a particular person or thing without naming or describing them
common 👁	/ˈkɒmən/	(adj)	happening often or existing in large numbers
culture 👁	/ˈkʌltʃə/	(n)	the way of life, especially customs and beliefs, of a group of people
endangered	/ɪnˈdeɪndʒəd/	(adj)	(of customs and traditions) in danger of being lost
exchange 👁	/ɪksˈtʃeɪndʒ/	(v)	to give something to someone, and receive something that they give you
expect 👁	/ɪkˈspekt/	(v)	to think that something will or should happen

Vocabulary	Pronunciation	Part of speech	Definition
formal 👁	/ˈfɔːməl/	(adj)	(of clothes, behaviour or language) serious or very polite
generation 👁	/ˌdʒenəˈreɪʃən/	(n)	all the people in a society or family who are approximately the same age
greet	/ɡriːt/	(v)	to welcome someone with particular words or actions
important 👁	/ɪmˈpɔːtənt/	(adj)	having a lot of power, influence or effect
obvious 👁	/ˈɒbviəs/	(adj)	easy to understand or see
preserve 👁	/prɪˈzɜːv/	(v)	to keep something the same, or prevent it from being damaged or destroyed
protection 👁	/prəˈtekʃən/	(n)	the act of keeping someone or something safe from injury, damage or loss
relationship 👁	/rɪˈleɪʃənʃɪp/	(n)	the way two people or groups feel and behave towards each other
separate 👁	/ˈsepərət/	(adj)	not joined or touching anything else
serious 👁	/ˈsɪəriəs/	(adj)	a serious problem or situation is bad and makes people worry
tradition 👁	/trəˈdɪʃən/	(n)	a belief or way of acting that people in a particular society or group have continued to follow for a long time

UNIT 5

Vocabulary	Pronunciation	Part of speech	Definition
active 👁	/ˈæktɪv/	(adj)	doing things which involve moving and using energy
advertising campaign	/ˈædvətaɪzɪŋ kæmˈpeɪn/	(n)	media projects to convince people to buy a product or change their behaviour
balanced diet	/ˌbælənst ˈdaɪət/	(n)	a daily eating programme which has a healthy mixture of different kinds of food

Vocabulary	Pronunciation	Part of speech	Definition
calories	/ˈkæləriz/	(n pl)	the measurement of the amount of energy found in food
campaign 👁	/kæmˈpeɪn/	(n)	a group of activities designed to motivate people to take action, such as giving money or changing their behaviour
educational programme	/ˌedʒuˈkeɪʃənəl ˈprəʊgræm/	(n)	classes or material to teach people about a particular topic
heart disease	/ˈhɑːt dɪˌziːz/	(n)	an illness of the heart
junk food	/ˈdʒʌŋk ˌfuːd/	(n)	food which is unhealthy but quick and easy to eat
life expectancy	/ˈlaɪf ɪkˌspektənsi/	(n)	how long a person can expect to live
moderate 👁	/ˈmɒdərət/	(adj)	not too much and not too little
nutritional 👁	/njuːˈtrɪʃən əl/	(adj)	relating to food and the way it affects your health
nutritional value	/njuːˈtrɪʃən əl ˈvæljuː/	(n)	how good a particular kind of food is for you
obesity	/əʊˈbiːsɪti/	(n)	the condition of weighing more than is healthy
physical activity	/ˈfɪzɪkəl ækˈtɪvəti/	(n)	moving around and doing things
portion 👁	/ˈpɔːʃən/	(n)	the amount of food served to one person
recognize 👁	/ˈrekəgnaɪz/	(v)	to understand; to accept that something is true
reduce 👁	/rɪˈdjuːs/	(v)	to limit; to use less of something
regular exercise	/ˈregjələ ˈeksəsaɪz/	(n)	sports or movement that people do at the same time each day, week, month, etc.
self-esteem	/ˌselfɪˈstiːm/	(n)	being confident and believing in yourself
serious 👁	/ˈsɪəriəs/	(adj)	bad or dangerous
serious illness	/ˈsɪəriəs ˈɪlnəs/	(n)	a very bad medical problem

Vocabulary	Pronunciation	Part of speech	Definition
UNIT 6			
artificial 👁	/ˌɑːtɪˈfɪʃəl/	(adj)	made by people; not in nature
break down	/breɪk daʊn/	(phr v)	to stop working, for example, a machine
dehumanize	/ˌdiːˈhjuːmənaɪz/	(v)	to remove from a person the special human qualities of independent thought, feeling for other people, etc.
disorganized	/dɪˈsɔːɡənaɪzd/	(adj)	not planned or organized well
electronic 👁	/ˌelekˈtrɒnɪk/	(adj)	sent or accessed by a computer or similar machine
enlarge	/ɪnˈlɑːdʒ/	(v)	to become bigger or to make something become bigger
equipment 👁	/ɪˈkwɪpmənt/	(n)	things that are used for a particular activity or purpose
essential 👁	/ɪˈsenʃəl/	(adj)	very important or necessary
harmful 👁	/ˈhɑːmfəl/	(adj)	able to hurt or damage
helpful 👁	/ˈhelpfəl/	(adj)	useful
illustrate 👁	/ˈɪləstreɪt/	(v)	to show the meaning or truth of something more clearly, especially by giving examples
movement 👁	/ˈmuːvmənt/	(n)	a change of position or place
object 👁	/ˈɒbdʒɪkt/	(n)	a thing you can see or touch that is not alive
pattern 👁	/ˈpætən/	(n)	a set of lines, colours or shapes which repeat in a regular way
personal 👁	/ˈpɜːsənəl/	(adj)	belonging to, or used by, just one person
prevent 👁	/prɪˈvent/	(v)	to stop something from happening or stop someone from doing something
rethink	/riːˈθɪŋk/	(v)	to change what you think about something or what you plan to do

Vocabulary	Pronunciation	Part of speech	Definition
three-dimensional	/ˌθriːdaɪˈmenʃənəl/	(adj)	not flat; having depth, length and width; 3D
translate	/trænzˈleɪt/	(v)	to change written or spoken words from one language to another
unlimited	/ʌnˈlɪmɪtɪd/	(adj)	without end or restriction
unsafe	/ʌnˈseɪf/	(adj)	dangerous

UNIT 7

Vocabulary	Pronunciation	Part of speech	Definition
advertising	/ˈædvətaɪzɪŋ/	(n)	the business of creating or sending out announcements in magazines, on television, etc. to attract shoppers
brand	/brænd/	(n)	the name of a product, or group of products, made by a company
collection	/kəˈlekʃən/	(n)	a group of new clothes produced by a fashion company
competitor	/kəmˈpetɪtə/	(n)	a business which tries to win or do better than other businesses selling almost the same products
conditions	/kənˈdɪʃənz/	(n pl)	the physical environment where people live or work
consumer	/kənˈsjuːmə/	(n)	a person who buys a product or service for their own use
cotton	/ˈkɒtən/	(n)	a plant used for making cloth, or the fabric made from the plant
designer label	/dɪˈzaɪnər ˈleɪbəl/	(n)	a company which makes or designs expensive clothes
import	/ɪmˈpɔːt/	(v)	to buy a product from another country and bring it into your country
invest	/ɪnˈvest/	(v)	to use money for the purpose of making a profit, for example, by building a factory
labour	/ˈleɪbə/	(n)	work

Vocabulary	Pronunciation	Part of speech	Definition
manufacture 👁	/ˌmænjəˈfæktʃə/	(v)	to make goods in a large quantity in a factory
manufacturing 👁	/ˌmænjəˈfæktʃərɪŋ/	(n)	the process of making things, especially in a factory
multinational	/ˌmʌltiˈnæʃənəl/	(adj)	referring to a business or company that has offices, stores or factories in several countries
offshore	/ɒfˈʃɔː/	(adj)	located in another country
outsource	/ˈaʊtsɔːs/	(v)	to have work done by another company, often in another country, rather than in your own company
overseas 👁	/ˌəʊvəˈsiːz/	(adv)	in, from, or to another country
season 👁	/ˈsiːzən/	(n)	a time of year when particular things happen
supplier	/səˈplaɪə/	(n)	a person or company that sells a product or service
textile	/ˈtekstaɪl/	(n)	cloth or fabric that is made by crossing threads under and over each other (by hand or machine)
volume 👁	/ˈvɒljuːm/	(n)	amount of something, especially when it is large
wage 👁	/weɪdʒ/	(n)	money that people earn for working

UNIT 8

consumer 👁	/kənˈsjuːmə/	(n)	a person who buys a product or service to use
demand 👁	/dɪˈmɑːnd/	(n)	the need for something to be sold or supplied
economy 👁	/iˈkɒnəmi/	(n)	the system by which a country produces and uses goods and money
employment 👁	/ɪmˈplɔɪmənt/	(n)	the fact of someone being paid to work for a company or organization

Vocabulary	Pronunciation	Part of speech	Definition
expenditure	/ɪkˈspendɪtʃə/	(n)	the total amount of money that a government or person spends on something
factor	/ˈfæktə/	(n)	one of the things that has an effect on a particular situation, decision, event, etc.
financial	/faɪˈnænʃəl/	(adj)	relating to money or how money is managed
income	/ˈɪnkʌm/	(n)	money that you earn by working, investing or producing goods
interest rate	/ˈɪntrəst ˌreɪt/	(n)	the percentage amount that you pay when you borrow money, or receive when you lend money, for a period of time
investment	/ɪnˈvestmənt/	(n)	something such as stocks or property which you buy in order to make a profit
investor	/ɪnˈvestə/	(n)	someone who puts money in a bank, business, etc. to make a profit
market	/ˈmɑːkɪt/	(n)	the total number of people who might want to buy something
percentage	/pəˈsentɪdʒ/	(n)	an amount of something, expressed as a number out of 100
poverty	/ˈpɒvəti/	(n)	the condition of being extremely poor
professional	/prəˈfeʃənəl/	(adj)	relating to work that needs special training or education
purchase	/ˈpɜːtʃəs/	(n)	something that you buy
recession	/rɪˈseʃən/	(n)	a period when the economy of a country is not doing well, but not as bad as a depression
return	/rɪˈtɜːn/	(n)	profit on money you have invested

Vocabulary	Pronunciation	Part of speech	Definition
revenue 👁	/ˈrevənjuː/	(n)	the income that a company or government receives
savings 👁	/ˈseɪvɪŋz/	(n pl)	money that you put away, usually in a bank, for a later date
standard of living	/ˌstændəd əv ˈlɪvɪŋ/	(n)	how much money and comfort someone has
stocks and shares	/stɒks ən ʃeəz/	(n)	parts of a publicly-owned business which can be bought and sold as investments
supply 👁	/səˈplaɪ/	(n)	an amount or quantity of something available to use
trend 👁	/trend/	(n)	the general direction of changes or developments
valuable 👁	/ˈvæljəbəl/	(adj)	worth a lot of money
value 👁	/ˈvæljuː/	(n)	how much money something could be sold for
wealthy 👁	/ˈwelθi/	(adj)	having lots of money or possessions; rich

VIDEO SCRIPTS

UNIT 1

▶ **Great egret and dolphin fishing**

Narrator: The marshes of South Carolina are the location of an interesting fish tale. There, these dolphins and egrets work together in a very special way.

These egrets are experts on the dolphins' behaviour.

The moment a dolphin comes to the surface of the water and checks the nearest mud bank, the birds get ready for action.

Then, it happens. The dolphins push the fish onto the shore.

When the fish are out of the water, the dolphins start eating. But the egrets also join them for dinner.

This is the only place in the world where you can see this kind of behaviour.

Strangely, the dolphins always use their right sides to push the fish to the shore.

The young dolphins learn this fishing technique from their parents, and so do the young egrets. Many of the birds now depend on the dolphins for their food. They never even fish for themselves.

These egrets and dolphins demonstrate the ability of different animal species to work together in order to survive.

UNIT 2

▶ **Colorado River, Grand Canyon, Yosemite**

Narrator: Some of the world's most beautiful natural environments are in the southwestern United States.

In just a few million years, the Colorado River has cut through parts of Arizona to form the Grand Canyon.

The Grand Canyon is 277 miles long and, in some places, 18 miles wide. At its deepest places, the river is a mile below the top of the canyon. It shows the effects of water and weather on the Earth's surface.

Its oldest rocks are almost two billion years old, nearly half the age of the Earth. This is the world's largest canyon, and the weather here can change dramatically. In the same day you can have hot, dry weather, followed by wind and snow. And every year the Colorado River cuts a little deeper into the bottom of the Grand Canyon.

Water also formed Carlsbad Caverns in New Mexico. Carlsbad is the largest, deepest cave system in North America. Even today water continues to change the inside of the caves.

The results are spectacular.

Finally, high in the Sierra Mountains of California is Yosemite National Park. Its famous landmark Half Dome was made by the frozen water in a glacier moving through the canyon. Today the glaciers are gone, but water from the melting mountain snow flows throughout the national park.

Yosemite Falls drops nearly 2,500 feet – it's the tallest waterfall in North America.

UNIT 3

▶ **The jumbo jet**

Narrator: In 1969, a true giant of the skies first took flight. It could cross the Atlantic with enough fuel and twice as many passengers as any airplane before it. Now, there are nearly 1,000 of them. Each one is able to fly over 14 hours to their destinations without stopping. It's the

747 – the jumbo jet – and this is the very first one.

Jimmy Barber helped build this very plane.

Jimmy Barber: Eight months straight you worked on the airplane, and we didn't just work, er, eight hours a day. Sometimes we worked 12 or more hours a day. And if it was necessary to sleep in your car in a parking lot, that's what you did. It was a highlight in my whole life was this aircraft, you know. Yeah.

Wow, this is great.

Narrator: This is the first time Jimmy has been aboard since he worked on it over 45 years ago.

Jimmy Barber: This is great.

Narrator: When it first flew, this was the most modern plane in the air. It was the first double-decker jet in history with a fancy first-class lounge upstairs. But it was the enormous space downstairs that changed commercial air travel forever. With room for around 500 people, it started the age of low-cost air travel.

Since its first flight, engineers have redesigned the 747 fifteen times. Today it flies further and faster than ever before.

UNIT 4

▶ South Korean Coming of Age Day

Narrator: In South Korea, as in many cultures around the world, a coming-of-age day is celebrated – a celebration of the age at which a person becomes an adult, and gains all the rights and responsibilities that go along with that. In South Korea, coming-of-age day is celebrated on the same day for everybody. It is held on the third Monday in May, for all 19-year-olds who will become 20-year-olds in the coming year.

In modern day South Korea, many celebrate the day by giving gifts of flowers. Parents or friends often give 20 roses – one for each year of the person's life. Perfume is another popular gift as it is not common for children to wear perfume. For South Koreans, perfume has a special meaning – giving perfume helps the new adult to become a person that people remember.

The modern coming-of-age day comes from a ceremony which dates back over 1,000 years – the hair-changing ceremony. For many years, the old ceremony was not very common. But, these days, it is again possible to take part in the traditional ceremony in many cities in South Korea. Young women do their hair in a chignon with *binyeo*, a jade hairpin. On their heads, they wear a *jokduri*, a kind of silk and wooden crown, covered with colourful decorations including enamel ornaments.

During the ceremony young men tie their hair under a net in a topknot. Later they will put on a hat made of bamboo and horsehair called a *gat*. The young people also learn how to put on the brightly-coloured, traditional, formal clothing known as *hanbok*. In fact, there are three different kinds of clothing ritual throughout the day.

This is an important day in every young Korean's life, as it is the day when they are independent for the first time, able to make decisions for themselves, drive and marry. The young adults bow to their parents. The parents bow in return and speak to their child of how proud they are of them as they become adults. For those who take part in the traditional ceremony, it is a day they will never want to forget.

UNIT 5

▶ **Sugar survey supports labelling on food and drinks**

Reporter: Six and a half pounds – that is the average monthly adult consumption of total sugars. Some of it comes naturally from the ingredients in our food, but a proportion is added by manufacturers. Now, the labels don't differentiate so we've done some of our own research. We found an *Alpen Trail Bar* has four teaspoons of sugar, of which almost a third is added, and *Nestlé* Munch Bunch drink has three teaspoons of sugar, we found more than two-thirds of that was added. This *Quaker Oat So Simple* porridge with fruits has four and a half teaspoons of sugar when made up with milk, and the company won't disclose how much of that is added. Manufacturers say labels are governed by EU rules, not their decisions, but the food industry is under pressure to reduce sugar. Sainsbury's says it's just reformulated some of its juices, but like other supermarkets, it's reluctant to act faster.

There is a widespread suspicion that the industry uses so much sugar 'cause it's a cheap ingredient and it makes products palatable.

Beth Hart: When you remove any food component that delivers flavour, um … you've got to do it slowly and gradually so you train the customer's palate to accept that change.

Reporter: But change is coming and campaigners are pinning their hopes on tomorrow's official report on sugar.

Katherine Jenner: We would be delighted to see a really good, strong recommendation from the scientific advisory board, um, ideally saying that sugar intake should be reduced to less than 5% of your daily, err … energy intake.

UNIT 6

▶ **China's man-made river**

Narrator: History is filled with stories of humans overcoming obstacles through discovery and invention. Take an enormous country like China. What do you do when most of your people live in the north, in cities like Beijing, but most of your water is in the south? You build an artificial river to bring water from the south to the north.

This river will be about 750 miles long when it is finished in 2030.

And this is it. A giant raised canal, or aqueduct – one of the largest engineering projects in the world.

Chinese workers and engineers are building the river piece by piece, in separate sections.

Each section starts as a metal framework. A team of 20 people build the metal frame.

Then the concrete is added.

Finally, the section is moved into place using one of the world's most powerful cranes.

Each section weighs 1,200 tons – more than three commercial airplanes.

This woman operates the crane. It's a very important job, and it takes great skill.

She must work very carefully so that each section of the artificial river is in the perfect position.

The water will flow north to Beijing without using any pumps.

So the end of each section must be exactly 1 centimetre lower than the other end.

When the river is finished and operating in 2030, the water from the south will reach millions of Chinese people in the north.

UNIT 7

▶ Savile Row's first female Master Tailor

Narrator: Savile Row – in the expensive area of Mayfair, London – is a street which is famous around the world for its top-quality men's suits. A two-piece suit made by hand by a Savile Row tailor involves at least 50 hours of work.

The suits made on Savile Row were traditionally for men, but women have always worked there, too. However, until now, no woman has made it to the top on Savile Row and become a master tailor.

Kathryn Sargent is the first female Master Tailor on Savile Row. Her new shop sells handmade suits for both men and women.

Interviewer: Ok, so ,err … Kathryn, how significant is it that you are the first woman to have her name above the door of a shop on Savile Row?

Kathryn Sargent: I just think it's a sign of the times really. I … there's far more women in the industry now. Erm … just behind the scenes, there have always been women present within the workrooms on Savile Row, but now, and now there's more women rising to some client-facing roles and more prominent positions within the trade, such as myself, as a business owner and as a head cutter. There's more, erm … women coming through as apprentices and actually over 65% of the newly qualified tailors last year were women.

Interviewer: Coming back to Savile Row is like a return home for you?

Kathryn Sargent: Absolutely, yeah. I grew up in this community, erm … I started here as a young graduate from college and, you know, trained at No. 1 Savile Row and was there for 15 years. Erm … as I said, we all know each other; it's a very small network and I've been very, sort of … encouraged and welcomed by the Savile Row Bespoke Association, and it's almost like coming home, and I'm one of them, so we all work in the same way with the same values and principles about our work. So, it's … you know, it's a great thing and it means a lot to me.

Interviewer: Not knowing much about the industry, I was surprised that there wasn't a female name on this street already; this very famous street already, that's, that's known worldwide. Are you hoping that what has happened today will see more female tailors coming in?

Kathryn Sargent: Absolutely, absolutely. And it's, you know, it's a mix of all sorts of different, erm … tailoring houses, some, you know, of the oldest ones have been here since the early 1800s so it's nice to be a new, erm … modern tailoring house with my name above the door. I think there will definitely be more women in the future potentially opening a business here.

UNIT 8

▶ The stock market crash of 1929

Narrator: On October 29, 1929, the New York Stock Exchange had its worst day ever – Black Tuesday. The stock market crashed, and investors lost billions of dollars in a single day. That day was the end of a decade of a strong US economy. It was the beginning of the Great Depression, the worst economic period in modern world history. During the next two years, stock prices fell 90%, banks and companies failed and millions of people around the world lost their jobs.

Today, you can visit the Museum of Financial History on Wall Street, in New York City, to learn more about what happened.

Man: So what we have here is the physical tape from October 29th, that Black Tuesday, and it's quite an important piece, it tells a great story.

Narrator: This is a replica of the machine that produced that ticker tape. The name *ticker tape* comes from the sound of the machine as it printed out the price of stocks and shares. But since the early 1970s, computers and electronic boards have reported the ups and downs in the stock market.

ACKNOWLEDGEMENTS

The authors and publishers acknowledge the following sources of copyright material and are grateful for the permissions granted. While every effort has been made, it has not always been possible to identify the sources of all the material used, or to trace all copyright holders. If any omissions are brought to our notice, we will be happy to include the appropriate acknowledgements on reprinting and in the next update to the digital edition, as applicable.

Key: T = Top, B = Below, L = Left, R = Right, BR = Below Right, BL = Below Left, B/G = Background, TL = Top Left, TC = Top Centre, TR = Top Right.

Text

Text on p. 32 adapted from 'Know the difference'. Copyright © Get Bear Smart Society. Reproduced with kind permission.

Photos

All below images are sourced from Getty Images.

pp. 14–15: WLDavies/E+; p. 19: Mark Newman/Lonely Planet Images; p. 23 (L): Ben Queenborough/Oxford Scientific; p. 23 (R): Marco Pozzi Photographer/Moment; p. 25: Miha Pavlin/Moment Select; p. 31: Jane Burton/Nature Picture Library; p. 32: ALBERTO GHIZZI PANIZZA/Science Photo Library; pp. 36–37: Kelly Cheng Travel Photography/Moment; p. 41: Maximilian Müller/Moment; p. 45: Minden Pictures; p. 48: Mint Images RF; pp. 58–59: Keren Su/The Image Bank; p. 62 (L): AFP; p. 62 (R): Bloomberg; p. 64: KARIM SAHIB/AFP; p. 67 (TL): Maksim Ozerov/Moment; p. 67 (TC): mammuth/E+; p. 67 (TR): Asanka Brendon Ratnayake/Lonely Planet Images; p. 67 (B/G): Gavin Hellier/robertharding; p. 71: Zoran Milich/Photonica; pp. 80–81: Mint Images – Art Wolfe/Mint Images RF; p. 86: NanoStockk/iStock/Getty Images Plus; p. 90 (L): Chung Sung-Jun/Getty Images News; p. 90 (R): Eye Ubiquitous/Universal Images Group; p. 91: ED JONES/AFP; p. 92: serts/E+; p. 98: Sven Hagolani; pp. 102–103: coberschneider/RooM; p. 106 (a): Zachary Miller/Image Source; p. 106 (b): Image Source; p. 106 (c): Kathrin Ziegler/Taxi/Getty Images; p. 106 (d): Resolution Productions/Blend Images; p. 106 (e): Ariel Skelley/DigitalVision; p. 106 (f): ViktorCap/iStock/Getty Images Plus; p. 106 (h): Tom M Johnson/Blend Images; p. 113: Andrew Fox/Corbis Documentary; pp. 124–125: Bloomberg; p. 129 (B/G): hooky13/iStock/Getty Images Plus; p. 129 (L): Clouds Hill Imaging Ltd./Corbis Documentary; p. 129 (R): Alex Wong/Getty Images News; p. 133 (T): Victor Habbick/Visuals Unlimited; p. 133 (BL): Koichi Kamoshida/Getty Images News; p. 133 (BR): Izusek/E+; pp. 146–147: Zero Creatives/Cultura; p. 151 (clothes): Timothy Hiatt/Getty Images Entertainment; p. 151 (Carmen): mangostock/iStock/Getty Images Plus; p. 151 (Ahmet): Jetta Productions/Blend Images; p. 152 (Jasmine): Atsushi Yamada/The Image Bank; p. 152 (Ben): Goodluz/iStock/Getty Images Plus; p. 152 (Sara): Jacob Wackerhausen/iStock/Getty Images; p. 152 (Fatima): Eugenio Marongiu/Cultura; p. 158: Richard Baker/Corbis News; pp. 168–169: VCG/Getty Images News; p. 173 (T): yodiyim/iStock/Getty Images Plus; p. 173 (B): Heritage Images/Hulton Archive.

The following image is sourced from other library:
p. 106 (g): Tom Wang/Alamy Stock Photo.

Front cover photography by Reimar Gaertner/UIG.

Video stills

All below stills are sourced from Getty Images.

p. 82 (video 1): Multi-bits/Image Bank Film; p. 82 (video 2): Malkovstock/Creatas Video+/Getty Images Plus; p. 82 (video 3, video 4): AFP Footage; p. 104, p. 148: ITN.

The following video stills are from other libraries
p. 16, p. 38, p. 60, p. 126, p. 170: BBC Worldwide Learning.

Illustrations

p. 27: Oxford Designers & Illustrators; p. 73: Simon Tegg.

Videos

All below clips are sourced from Getty Images and BBC Worldwide Learning.

AFP Footage; topnatthapon/Creatas Video; kickimages/Creatas Video+/Getty Images Plus; Faithfulshot; ITN; Sky News/Film Image Partner; Tribune Broadcasting – Fabiola Franco; ITN; Wazee Archiva/Archive Films: Editorial; Roger Maynard – Footage; Press association; Bloomberg Video – Footage/Bloomberg; Feature Story News – Footage/Getty Images Editorial Footage; Crane.tv – Footage/Getty Images Editorial Footage; BBC Motion Gallery Editorial/BBC News; Skyworks Places/Image Bank Film; Gorlov/Creatas Video+/Getty Images Plus; Multi-bits/Image bank film; BBC Worldwide Learning.

Corpus

Development of this publication has made use of the Cambridge English Corpus (CEC). The CEC is a multi-billion word computer database of contemporary spoken and written English. It includes British English, American English and other varieties of English. It also includes the Cambridge Learner Corpus, developed in collaboration with the University of Cambridge ESOL Examinations. Cambridge University Press has built up the CEC to provide evidence about language use that helps to produce better language teaching materials.

Cambridge Dictionaries

Cambridge dictionaries are the world's most widely used dictionaries for learners of English. The dictionaries are available in print and online at dictionary.cambridge.org. Copyright © Cambridge University Press, reproduced with permission.

Typeset by emc design ltd.

UNLOCK SECOND EDITION ADVISORY PANEL

"The videos capture students' attention and provide a good introduction to the topic."

"Students are encouraged to think critically to build their English language and academic skills."

"It's what our students need to help them move on into their Academic courses."

"I think the new Teacher's development pack content is very attractive and informative."

Mexico · UK · Turkey · Palestine · Russia · Qatar · UAE · Oman · Saudi Arabia · China · Japan · Australia

We would like to thank the following ELT professionals all around the world for their support, expertise and input throughout the development of *Unlock* Second Edition:

Adnan Abu Ayyash, Birzeit University, Palestine	Takayuki Hara, Kagoshima University, Japan	Megan Putney, Dhofar University, Oman
Bradley Adrain, University of Queensland, Australia	Esengül Hasdemir, Atilim University, Turkey	Wayne Rimmer, United Kingdom
Sarah Ali, Nottingham Trent International College (NTIC), United Kingdom	Irina Idilova, Moscow Institute of Physics and Technology, Russia	Sana Salam, TED University, Turkey
Ana Maria Astiazaran, Colegio Regis La Salle, Mexico	Meena Inguva, Sultan Qaboos University, Oman	Setenay Şekercioglu, Işık University, Turkey
Asmaa Awad, University of Sharjah, United Arab Emirates	Vasilios Konstantinidis, Prince Sultan University, Kingdom of Saudi Arabia	Robert B. Staehlin, Morioka University, Japan
Jesse Balanyk, Zayed University, United Arab Emirates	Andrew Leichsenring, Tamagawa University, Japan	Yizhi Tang, Xueersi English, TAL Group, China
Lenise Butler, Universidad del Valle de México, Mexico	Alexsandra Minic, Modern College of Business and Science, Oman	Valeria Thomson, Muscat College, Oman
Esin Çağlayan, Izmir University of Economics, Turkey	Daniel Newbury, Fuji University, Japan	Amira Traish, University of Sharjah, United Arab Emirates
Matthew Carey, Qatar University, Qatar	Güliz Özgürel, Yaşar University, Turkey	Poh Leng Wendelkin, INTO City, University of London, United Kingdom
Eileen Dickens, Universidad de las Américas, Mexico	Özlem Perks, Istanbul Ticaret University, Turkey	Yoee Yang, The Affiliated High School of SCNU, China
Mireille Bassam Farah, United Arab Emirates	Claudia Piccoli, Harmon Hall, Mexico	Rola Youhia, University of Adelaide College, Australia
Adriana Ghoul, Arab American University, Palestine	Tom Pritchard, University of Edinburgh, United Kingdom	Long Zhao, Xueersi English, TAL Group, China
Burçin Gönülsen, Işık University, Turkey		